The Home Café

Creative Recipes for Espresso, Matcha,
Tea and Coffee Drinks

Asia Lui Chapa

Creator of AC Home Café

PAGE STREET
PUBLISHING CO.

PAGE STREET
PUBLISHING CO.

For my "Grama," Rosemary D. Lui

My inspiration and moral compass. She was the most creative person
I've ever known and always filled the house with love, warmth and fun.

For my Dad, Eric A. Chapa

My loving father and constant comfort even from afar.
He was the best of the best and never failed to put a smile
on your face when you needed it.

Cheers to you, Grama and Dad. This one is for you.

7 *Introduction*

9 Home Café Must-Haves

10 Espresso Tools

12 Coffee Tools

14 Tea Tools

17 Fun Extras

19 You Had Me at Espresso

20 The Classic Latte

23 Tres Leches Iced Latte

24 Frozen Horchata Latte

28 Almond Brûlée Latte

31 Warm & Toasty White Mocha

32 Tiramisù Espresso con Panna

35 Brown Sugar Banana Latte

36 Cherry Pistachio Mocha

39 Cinnamon Choco-Latte Float

40 Shaken Maple Espresso

43 Toasted Coconut Affogato

44 Wake Up, Lavender

47 Espresso Tónica

48 Sparkling Espresso Lemonade

51 Coffee, Coffee and More Coffee

52 The Classic Drip Coffee

55 The Classic Cold Brew

56 Spiced Honey Coffee

59 Foamy Spiced Maple Café

60 Honeycomb Coffee

63 Salty Maple Cold Brew Granita

66 Campfire Iced Coffee

69 Shaken White Mocha Iced Coffee

70 Ube Coffee Float

73 Cheese Foam Iced Coffee

74 Cookies 'n' Cream Coffee

77 Gingerbread Cold Brew

78 Honey Lavender Cold Brew

81 Be Bold Brew

83 More Matcha Please

84 Matcha-Misù Tea Latte

87 Spiced Maple Matcha

88 La Vie En Rose Latte

91 Double Chocolate Matcha Float

92 Mixed Berry Bubbly Matcha

95 The Lemongrass Lady

Table of Contents

96   Icy Guava Matcha

99   Sparkling Matcha Lemonade

100   The Bright Side

103   Hey, Hot-Tea

104   Blueberry Lavender Tea Latte

107   Honey, Do You Like Sesame?

110   Jasmine Tea Horchatte

113   The Vegan Thai Iced Tea

114   The Sunnyside

117   The Earl of Grapefruit

118   Tea Berry Affogato

121   Mango Tango Tea

123   Green Tea Delights

124   My Floral Lady

127   The Winter Tropicale

128   Strawbasil Float

131   Ombré Green Tea Granita

132   Passionate About Green Tea

135   Herbal Infusions

136   Corazón del Sol

139   A Fresh Start

140   Sleepytime Soda

143   Pretty in Purple

144   A Ginger Swig

147   Home Café Happy Hour

148   Good Morning, Tommy C.

151   The Salted Caramel-Tini

155   The Magic Margarita

159   Café Disco

160   The Mythical Mojito

163   Acknowledgments

164   About the Author

165   Index

Introduction

An ice-cold glass of water. A warm mug of your favorite tea. That piping hot cup of coffee. The drinks you get with friends after work. If you couldn't already tell, I think drinks are pretty cool. Growing up in a healthy-eating household, the weekends were very special to me. That's when I was allowed to have drinks that weren't milk or water. I would eagerly await my hot chocolate on Saturday mornings, and the possibility of having a soda or lemonade when eating out thrilled me to no end. Even now as an adult, I get genuinely excited just thinking about what my next drink will be.

My love for drinks and creative food in general is part of the reason I took such a liking to "home café" videos on Instagram, a trend that originally became popular in South Korea, Japan and China. In March 2020, I had just been laid off from my part-time job while finishing up my master's degree and was super stressed with all of the uncertainty of the year. I found solace in home café accounts on TikTok and Instagram, like @y.na__ and @hanse___. It was something I had never seen before when it came to drinks—intricate ice shapes, colorful liquids and pure fun. So, on day three of the world's first collective quarantine, I attempted to film my first home café video. From then on, I began posting videos on TikTok and eventually took to Instagram to create @ac_homecafé, focusing on how-tos and later on, recipes! From posting simple videos online to partnering with brands to showcase their products, the home café trend has become such an important part of my life, and I hope it can become part of yours, as well. To me it's more than just making a coffee or pouring a glass of lemonade. It's about being able to create something, no matter how simple.

This book is for anyone who loves drinks or wants to elevate their current coffee or tea game a bit, or anyone who wants to test the home café process out. I know it may sound hard or like it's too much work—that's what I thought, too. I promise that making drinks at home is much more fun and a lot more affordable than you think, and you get to customize everything to your preference! You don't like your drink too sweet? Add as much or as little sweetener as you want. Do you like strong coffee? Make it *strong*. Want to save some money? We can make that happen.

The recipes in the chapters to come have been crafted with you, The Coffee Lover, The Tea Lover, The On-The-Go-Getter and The Curious in mind. From espresso to matcha to cocktails, you can make them *all* and in the comfort of your own home. Not only is it more affordable than drinking out every day, but it is *actually* doable. Want to build your own home café? Let's get started!

Home Café Must-Haves

This chapter will equip you with all you need to know about building your own home café. When I first started crafting my own home café recipes, there was so much trial and error. I've learned a lot since then, and I'm excited to share that knowledge here with you. If you don't know where to start when it comes to espresso, coffee, matcha or tea in general, don't worry. I'll break down the different ways to brew espresso at home, how to get that coffee shop milk foam in your kitchen and let you in on some tips for the perfect matcha shot!

A common misconception about home café is that everything has to be made from scratch . . . and that could not be further from the truth. Yes, you are making drinks at home, but that doesn't mean you'll be sequestered to the kitchen for hours on end. You'll get some insight on some of the shortcuts you can use in your home without sacrificing quality or time.

I must admit, half of the appeal of home café is the aesthetic and the life-style element of doing things your way. So, this chapter ends with some tips for fun extras that make your recipes that much fancier and more fun to drink. I hope this chapter opens your eyes to all the possibilities that a little slice of life (like drinks) has to offer.

Espresso Tools

Moka Pots

The moka pot (pictured on the left), a staple in European and Latin American kitchens for making morning espresso, is one of the most affordable and convenient ways to make espresso at home. All you have to do is add water to the base, put espresso grounds in its basket, put it on the stove and let it brew. From taking the moka pot out of your cabinet to pouring your espresso shot, the process takes about 10 minutes at most. A con to this method is that the moka pot does not provide espresso with the "crema" (that creamy light brown goodness that professional machines provide) on top when brewing. But some pros to this method are that you can find moka pots in-store or online for anywhere from $7 to $30, and the cleanup is super quick. This method will make a speedy, quality shot of espresso. You cannot go wrong with the OG moka pot.

Fancier Espresso Machines

Let's be realistic . . . not everyone has a professional-grade espresso machine. So, when I say "fancier espresso machines," I mean any machine that isn't a moka pot. If you have a professional setup like one you'd find in a restaurant, then quite frankly I am jealous. I have heard that (on rare occasions) you can find professional espresso machines at thrift stores. The reality is that us home baristas can't always acquire those professional tools, either because they are too expensive, don't fit into our kitchens or are simply too hard to find, and that's okay. There are a myriad of other elevated espresso makers that will get the job done and done well. While espresso experts may shy away from using automatic espresso machines because of the quality or the lack of manually pulling a shot of espresso by hand, a Nespresso (pictured on the right), an illy, a Lavazza or a Smeg will still provide you with a piping hot, strong shot of espresso with that illustrious crema on top.

Milk Frothers

While a bare, no-frills shot of espresso is something to be marveled at, a common accompaniment is milk. Cow milk, oat, soy, almond, coconut, pistachio, cashew, macadamia nut, pea . . . you name it. Since most hot espresso drinks involve milk or a milk foam of some sort, a great way to make milk foam at home is with an electric handheld frother (pictured in

the middle), a standing milk frother or the steam wand on an espresso machine, all of which you can find at most places that stock kitchen supplies like Target or Walmart and, of course, online. The most convenient option is an electric handheld frother. Most are powered by batteries and require very minimal cleanup. The electric handheld is my personal favorite because they are the most affordable of all the options and only take up a little bit of counter or drawer space. Portable frothers usually take anywhere from 30 seconds to 1 minute to get that expert froth on your milk, but may take longer for some non-dairy milks like almond or oat. Whichever frother you choose, make sure it fits your taste and your lifestyle.

Coffee Tools

Drip Coffee Makers

Drip coffee makers are the most common coffee appliance . . . in America, at least. You or someone you know probably has one in their house right now. The ones you find in-store are automatic, which makes them great for everyday use. There are even some that you prep the night before and program to start the next morning. They come in many different colors and styles, but it is hard to go wrong with one of these. My personal favorite thing about electric drip coffee makers (pictured above on the right) is that they will do all the work for you. They will heat up your water, pour it over the grounds and keep the pot of coffee warm after brewing. Whichever brand of electric drip machine you choose, this is an affordable and quick way to make coffee every morning.

Pour-Over Sets

A pour-over coffee set (pictured on the left) is another great way to brew coffee at home. With the at-home coffee game on the rise, there are plenty more tools that make creating drinks much easier. For this method you will need a cup or heat-safe pitcher to catch the coffee, the pour-over basket and a coffee filter. If you buy a pour-over set, these tools will come together in a tidy kit, so not to worry. First, you'll heat up the water, line the basket with a filter and add your coffee grounds. You can grind your own beans or use your favorite store-bought grounds for this step. Once your water is heated up, you'll pour it over the grounds slowly and the coffee will drip into the pitcher or cup below and *voilà* . . . you have a pour-over!

French Press

The French press (pictured in the middle) is another convenient way to brew your coffee. All you'll need is some hot water, coffee grounds and the French press. In this method, you heat up the water, add your coffee grounds and pour in the hot water to fill the press. After you let it steep for anywhere from 3 to 8 minutes depending on the type of grind you use (less for medium grounds and longer for coarse grounds), you can *press* down the filter and serve as usual. This method is different from the drip and pour-over methods in that instead of a constant stream of water passing through the coffee grounds, the water and coffee harmoniously sit together during brewing.

Store-Bought Iced Coffee & Cold Brew

If you prefer to make your own iced coffee, you can use the drip method, pour-over method or French press method and let it chill in the refrigerator or freezer. There is also a cold brew recipe on page 55 if you want to add that to your repertoire. If you'd rather skip the at-home brewing altogether, grocery stores and even some coffee shops now stock a huge assortment of different pre-made iced coffees, cold brews and coffee concentrates. Whether you're making it at home or buying it pre-made, you have options, so do what works!

Tea Tools

Tea Kettle

A tea kettle (pictured in the middle) is for more than just tea! While its most basic purpose is to heat up the water for your tea, it is also great for pour-over coffee . . . and anything else you need hot water for. There are stovetop tea kettles, electric kettles and gooseneck kettles, which are ideal for pour-overs because of the length and precision of the spout. Getting a tea kettle will undeniably elevate your home café.

Tea Infusers

Tea infusers (pictured on the left) are another staple tea tool, especially if you like making your own tea blends or using loose leaf teas. They come in "basket" forms, spoon forms and there are even some teapots with built-in tea infusers. Whether you are brewing your tea hot or cold, tea infusers allow you to control the strength and combinations of flavors and are environmentally friendly!

Matcha Whisk

If you like matcha, are curious about matcha or don't know where to start with matcha, begin with a matcha whisk (pictured on the right). It is the single most important tool for authentic, smooth-tasting tea. Because matcha powder is so finely ground, the slender and delicate prongs of the bamboo matcha whisk work to break down every clump to make the tea perfectly foamy. I've tried mixing matcha with a frother instead of a whisk and it's *not* the same. If you like matcha and want to add it to your home café menu, put the matcha whisk at the top of your list.

Fun Extras

Some of the most enjoyable parts of home café are the fun extras. Yes, you could use any ice cube tray or any old glass, but it's fun to experiment with different ice shapes and sizes and different glasses from time to time. Want to drink your coffee out of a wine glass? *Do it.* Do you want to see little, tiny heart-shaped ice while drinking a matcha lemonade? You can! Whatever extras you choose, have fun with it and let your heart guide the way.

Ice Molds

Ice is a much bigger part of your home café than you might think. If you are in it for the aesthetics, the most pleasing molds tend to be the tiny cubes, tiny spheres and other unique shapes like hearts, flowers and animals. I get most of my ice molds on Amazon, Tovolo or other kitchen supply websites, but there are lots of options at grocery stores and home supply stores like Target, Bed Bath & Beyond, IKEA and Daiso.

Glassware

Half of the fun of home café is choosing your glass. Glasses have become such mundane items, so I challenge you to find the beauty in the glasses that are already in your cupboard. Do you see any potential? How about that one glass that you never use? Would iced tea or iced coffee look good in it? You might be surprised!

If you're in the market for new glasses, some of the coolest places to buy glassware are from thrift stores, dollar stores, IKEA, Michaels, JOANN Fabric & Craft Stores and Target. While any place that sells glassware is an option, some of the greatest finds come from thrift stores. I can't tell you how many unique and vintage glasses I've found while perusing the aisles. I'd say about 50 percent of the glasses in the pages to come are thrifted! Whether you find a new love for a forgotten glass or are procuring a new glassware collection for your home café, the most important thing is that each piece brings you unquestionable joy.

You Had Me at *Espresso*

Espresso. That rich, toasty brown sip that remedies a morning yawn. The yin to milk's yang. Espresso is brewed from coffee beans and their grounds, but gets its unique name from how you brew it: hot water pressed through coffee grounds at high pressure.

What do you think of when you hear the word espresso? I think of those tiny little cups filled with piping hot, dark brown coffee. I remember asking my mom for one of those tiny drinks as a kid, obviously not knowing what it was, to which she laughed and explained that I probably wouldn't like it and, "It'll stunt your growth! Do you want to be short like me?" Many years later, espresso is one of my favorite morning treats . . . I am short, though.

For a long time, I thought that anything with espresso seemed too fancy or too complicated to make at home. That assumption is partly correct because when we look at an espresso setup in any local coffee shop, it can be intimidating: the type of beans, having to weigh them, grind them and press them before loading them into a contraption that provides 1 ounce (30 ml) of heavenly espresso. But as you saw in the Espresso Tools section (page 10), there are lots of simpler brewing methods that we can use in our home cafés.

This chapter explores the different preparations of espresso, from the classic latte, to mochas, to affogatos and even citrus pairings. All 14 recipes have different inspirations, but the goal for each was the same: to open your eyes to all that espresso has to offer. From the warm and toasty pairings of cinnamon and cardamom, to the unique fruity flavors of coconut and cherry and the more outlandish combos like espresso and sparkling water, you are in for some fun caffeinated combinations!

The Classic Latte

1 serving

The humble latte—in its most basic form—is a layering of espresso, steamed milk and milk foam. The deep, roasted flavor of the espresso paired with the creaminess of the milk makes it the ideal morning sip or afternoon pick-me-up. While it is delicious as is, it's also the perfect coffee canvas for spices, syrups and sweeteners. And if you're feeling fancy, you can even try to create some latte art of your own . . . that's a skill I just haven't mastered yet!

2 oz (60 ml) freshly brewed espresso
6 oz (180 ml) milk of choice (I recommend oat)
Ice (optional)

Begin by brewing your espresso. For less cleanup, you can brew the espresso directly into your cup. While that's brewing, start to steam the milk. If you have a professional espresso machine you can use its steam wand, but if your home café is lacking an expert espresso machine (like mine), you can steam your milk on the stovetop over medium-high heat until it comes to a light boil, or put your milk in the microwave for 2 minutes.

Once steamed, froth your milk according to the directions for your handheld frother, standing frother or espresso machine. Pour your espresso into your cup (if you didn't brew directly into it) and follow with the steamed milk. The milk foam should come out last to top off your drink.

Home Café Tip

If you're in an iced coffee mood, skip the steaming and frothing and add ice to your milk and espresso.

Tres Leches Iced Latte

1 serving

This decadent sip is inspired by one of my favorite desserts, tres leches cake! The classic dessert is a yellow cake soaked in "tres leches," or "three milks," comprised of sweetened condensed milk, evaporated milk and whole milk. The milks in this latte are sweetened condensed milk, the milk of choice for your latte and whipped cream. Whether you're curious about tasting tres leches cake or it's one of your all-time favorites, this latte is a must-try.

2 oz (60 ml) freshly brewed espresso

1–2 tbsp (15–30 ml) sweetened condensed milk

6 oz (180 ml) milk of choice (I recommend oat or coconut)

2 oz (60 ml) heavy cream

1 tbsp (15 g) granulated sugar, or to taste (optional)

Ice

A sprinkle of cinnamon and/or cinnamon stick, for garnish

Begin by brewing your espresso. In your glass, add the sweetened condensed milk and milk of choice and mix them until they are well combined. In a separate bowl, combine the heavy cream and sugar (if using) and whisk or froth them until the mixture becomes thick and spoonable.

To your milk mixture, add the ice and your fresh espresso. To get the layered effect, slowly pour the espresso over an ice cube or over the back of a spoon. Top your latte with a generous dollop of whipped cream and sprinkle with ground cinnamon, a cinnamon stick or both.

Home Café Tip

For a vegan, non-dairy alternative, substitute the sweetened condensed milk for condensed coconut milk and heavy cream for coconut cream.

Frozen Horchata Latte

1 serving + 6 servings horchata

Horchata was the best treat growing up. Mexican horchata is made with "arroz," or rice, when compared to the Spanish horchata made with "chufas," or tiger nuts. This recipe uses the classic horchata *de arroz* as a foundation for espresso and cinnamon whipped cream. If you've never tried horchata before, it is creamy, complex and an instant comfort.

Horchata

1 cup (185 g) uncooked white rice (I recommend long grain or jasmine)

2 cinnamon sticks

32 oz (960 ml) warm water

8 oz (240 ml) milk of choice (I recommend 2% milk or any non-dairy alternative)

A splash of vanilla extract

12 oz (360 ml) cold water

¾ cup (150 g) granulated sugar, or to taste

Frozen Latte

2 oz (60 ml) freshly brewed espresso

2 oz (60 ml) heavy cream

1 tbsp (15 g) granulated sugar, or to taste (optional)

A dash of ground cinnamon, plus more for garnish

6 oz (180 ml) Horchata (store-bought will work too)

¾ cup (170 g) ice

Start your drink prep by making your horchata. If you're using store-bought, you can skip this step. Begin by washing your rice until the water is almost clear. Once clean, put the rice, cinnamon sticks and warm water into a blender and let it soak in the fridge overnight for at least 8 hours. When the rice and cinnamon are done soaking, blend your mixture until it's smooth. Then, strain it to get out the bigger pieces of cinnamon and rice. To your *agua de arroz*, or rice water, add the milk, vanilla extract and cold water. Last, add the sugar little by little, tasting as you go to find your perfect sweetness. After making your latte, store the remaining horchata in a sealed jar or container in the fridge for 3 to 5 days.

(continued)

Frozen Horchata Latte *(continued)*

Begin making your frozen latte by brewing your espresso. While that is brewing, make your cinnamon whipped cream. In a cup, combine your heavy cream, sugar (if using) and cinnamon. You can whisk your mixture with an electric handheld frother, electric beater or a normal whisk until it reaches your desired consistency. I like to whip mine until it forms stiff peaks.

Next, to a blender, add your horchata, espresso and ice and blend it until it transforms into an icy light brown color. To assemble your drink, add your ice-blended horchata latte to your cup and top it with your cinnamon whipped cream. Last, top off your frozen latte with a couple dashes of ground cinnamon.

Home Café Tip

You can make your whipped cream ahead of time and store it in the fridge for up to 2 days to have it ready whenever you are.

Almond Brûlée Latte

1 serving

The warmth of the sun during golden hour, the screams of kids on a roller coaster in the distance, the hum of hungry attendees ordering their favorite carnival snacks . . . carnival snacks. This recipe was inspired by one of my favorites: the sweet and salty candied almonds that come in the instantly recognizable checkered cones. The ones that come fresh out of the kettle and stay warm until you take your first taste. Now that's what I'm talking about! The almond extract, brown sugar and pinch of sea salt combined with the espresso in this recipe will transport you to the first bite of that beloved carnival classic.

2 oz (60 ml) freshly brewed espresso
6 oz (180 ml) milk of choice (I recommend almond)
1 tbsp (15 g) brown sugar, plus more for garnish
½ tsp almond extract
A pinch of sea salt

Begin by brewing your espresso. While that is brewing, you can start to heat up your milk with a steamer, on the stove over medium-high heat until it comes to a light boil or in the microwave for 2 minutes. To your mug, add the brown sugar, almond extract, salt and your espresso shot, stirring the ingredients until they are all combined.

Once your milk is steamed, froth it for 30 to 45 seconds. Next, pour your frothed milk into your cup over the espresso mixture. Watch as the dark brown color of the espresso turns into a milky almond color. The foamy milk should come out last, topping your latte ever so delicately. Garnish your latte with an extra sprinkle of brown sugar for an instant brûlée effect.

Warm & Toasty White Mocha

1 serving

White chocolate isn't just for macadamia nut cookies anymore. To be honest, I think white chocolate gets a bit of a bad rap, *but* it has become loved in the coffee world. The creamy richness of white chocolate combined with espresso is now a highly requested duo. A spin on the classic white mocha latte, this recipe adds a bit of cardamom into the mix, making it slightly smoky and aromatic. It'll make you go "What *is* that?" but in the best way.

2 oz (60 ml) freshly brewed espresso
6 oz (180 ml) milk of choice (I recommend almond or pistachio)
1 tbsp (15 ml) white mocha sauce, plus more for garnish
A couple dashes ground cardamom, plus more for garnish

Begin by brewing your espresso into your cup. While that is brewing, you can start to heat up your milk with a steamer, on the stove over medium-high heat until it comes to a light boil or in the microwave for 2 minutes. Then, add your white mocha sauce to the espresso in your mug, followed by the ground cardamom. Stir these ingredients together until they're well combined.

Once your milk is steamed, froth it or add it to your espresso as is. It's completely up to you. I suggest frothing it for at least 30 seconds to make sure you get that nice layer of foam on top. After adding the milk to your mug, you can top it with another drizzle of white mocha sauce and a sprinkle of ground cardamom.

Home Café Tip

There are a lot of different chocolate sauce options to choose from when building your own home café. You can always use white chocolate chips and melt them until they are drizzle-able, or you can sample some store-bought sauces found in almost any grocery store near you. My favorite store-bought options are Torani and Ghirardelli white mocha sauces.

Tiramisù Espresso con Panna

1 serving

This lovely twist on the classic Italian dessert is tantalizingly delicious. While the original dessert recipe uses lady fingers as a base, this recipe flips that notion on its head by making espresso the star of the show. Mascarpone cheese is used as a tart contrast to bring the drink together seamlessly. Whether you're drinking this in the morning or serving it as a dessert to family and friends, they'll be sure to be caffeinated and satisfied.

1 tbsp (15 g) granulated sugar, or to taste (optional)

1 tsp mascarpone cheese

1 oz (30 ml) heavy cream

2 oz (60 ml) freshly brewed espresso

1 tsp unsweetened cocoa powder, for garnish

2 lady fingers, for garnish (optional)

Begin by making your mascarpone "panna." Add the granulated sugar (if using) and mascarpone to a bowl. Because mascarpone is thick, it can be hard to combine with the heavy cream, so we want to mix the sugar and mascarpone together until they become soft, then add in the heavy cream. You can even combine the heavy cream little by little to make sure the panna comes out silky smooth. Whisk the panna until it becomes scoopable, but not so stiff that it can't slide off your spoon.

When you're done whisking, give your arm a little break and brew your espresso. I suggest brewing it straight into your cup for less cleanup. Next, top your espresso shot with a generous spoonful of your mascarpone panna. Garnish your coffee with the cocoa powder, just like the classic tiramisù. Serve up your espresso con panna with a few lady fingers (if desired) for a deconstructed tiramisù experience.

Brown Sugar Banana Latte

1 serving

Have you ever had banana milk? I hadn't until about 2 years ago. When I had it, I was . . . perplexed and curious. Honestly, I didn't really like it that much. But after lots of fails and finally a triumph, we have the downright delicious brown sugar banana milk iced latte. It takes the familiarity of a bananas foster dessert and transforms it into a subtly flavored banana latte. You could always use banana essence, but the bananas combined with brown sugar make the perfect pair for a homemade syrup.

Brown Sugar Banana Syrup

½ cup (100 g) brown sugar

4 oz (120 ml) water

A pinch of sea salt

½ banana, sliced

Latte

2 oz (60 ml) chilled espresso

Brown Sugar Banana Syrup, to taste

Ice

8 oz (240 ml) milk of choice (I recommend 2% or any non-dairy alternative)

Begin your drink prep by making your brown sugar banana syrup. Add the brown sugar, water, sea salt and banana slices to a small saucepan over medium heat. Stir your mixture often until the brown sugar dissolves and the bananas begin to soften. Once the sugar dissolves completely, turn the heat to low and let the syrup simmer for 5 to 7 minutes. While it's simmering, you can mash your bananas if you want your syrup to have more of a texture. If you want your syrup to be smooth, don't mash! When it's done simmering, take the syrup off the heat, strain it and let it cool. Once cooled, store the syrup in an airtight container in the fridge for up to 5 days.

Next, brew your espresso and stick it in the freezer for a few minutes, or let it sit out to chill slightly. This will prevent the hot espresso from diluting your latte.

To your glass, add the banana syrup, ice and milk. Top the banana milk with your chilled espresso, slowly pouring it over an ice cube or the back of a spoon.

Cherry Pistachio Mocha

1 serving

Chocolate, cherries, coffee and . . . pistachios? I found inspiration for this recipe while sipping on espresso and eating a big slice of Black Forest cake. I love Black Forest cake, but it was missing a little bit of texture, so *ding!* pistachios came to mind. The bitter and sweet mocha and nuttiness of the pistachios in this recipe work to balance the tart cherry for a truly mouthwatering and well-rounded experience.

Cherry Pistachio Syrup

¼ cup (35 g) cherries, fresh or frozen
¼ cup (25 g) pistachios, chopped
¼ cup (50 g) granulated sugar
2 oz (60 ml) water

Mocha

2 oz (60 ml) freshly brewed espresso
1 tsp unsweetened cocoa powder
Cherry Pistachio Syrup, to taste
Ice
8 oz (240 ml) milk of choice
(I recommend 2% or any non-dairy alternative)

Start your drink prep by making your cherry pistachio syrup. In a small saucepan over medium heat, add the cherries, pistachios, granulated sugar and water. Stir your mixture often until the sugar dissolves and the cherries soften. As you're stirring, make sure to mash your cherries to release their flavor and help make your syrup a rich red color. Turn the heat to low and let your syrup simmer for 5 to 7 minutes. Once simmered and slightly thickened, take the syrup off the heat and strain out the cherry and pistachio pieces. Let the syrup cool to room temperature and store it in an airtight container in the fridge for up to 1 week.

Next, brew your espresso, and while it's still hot, stir in your cocoa powder to create a mocha shot. To your glass, add the cherry pistachio syrup, ice and milk. You can stir your cherry milk mixture and watch as your milk turns a light pink color. Last, top your milk with your mocha shot by slowly pouring it over an ice cube into your glass if you want to create that layered look.

Cinnamon Choco-Latte Float

1 serving

This recipe is inspired by the famous Abuelita chocolate my cousins and I would drink on Christmas morning. One sip, and I'm right back to those memories of us wearing our PJs and taking turns opening presents around the tree. For a long time, these were flavors that I reserved for holidays and special occasions, but if there's anything I've learned, it's to seize the moment and enjoy the little things that bring you joy . . . with a shot of espresso, of course! This comforting combination of chocolate and cinnamon is an ode to the cozy memories of my childhood. It will awaken your senses, and its subtle decadence makes it the perfect treat to enjoy all year round.

2 oz (60 ml) freshly brewed espresso
A dash of ground cinnamon, plus more for garnish (optional)
6 oz (180 ml) milk of choice (I recommend oat or coconut)
Ice (optional)
1 scoop chocolate ice cream
Cinnamon stick, for garnish (optional)

Begin by brewing your espresso. In your cup, combine the ground cinnamon and milk of choice and mix well. To this cinnamon milk mixture, add the ice (if you're in an iced coffee mood) and espresso.

Top off your coffee with a generous scoop of chocolate ice cream. If you'd like, garnish with a sprinkle of ground cinnamon or a cinnamon stick (or both, if desired) and enjoy!

Home Café Tip

The hydrophobic nature of ground cinnamon can make it difficult to combine with liquids. When combining the milk and cinnamon, use a frother or small whisk to eliminate clumping.

Shaken Maple Espresso

1 serving

When I think of this recipe, I think of pure fun. It may be because I like espresso, or it may be because I like shaking things, but it's mostly because it is amazingly delicious. Whatever your reason for trying this recipe, let it be for the enjoyment you'll get from shaking it and the smile from the ensuing "ahhhh" after your first sip.

3 oz (90 ml) chilled espresso
Ice
1–2 tbsp (15–30 ml) maple syrup
A pinch of sea salt
1 oz (30 ml) milk of choice

Start by brewing your espresso. Once it's brewed, stick it in the freezer for a few minutes or let it sit out to cool slightly. This will prevent the hot espresso from diluting the ice too much.

To a mason jar or cocktail shaker, add the espresso, ice, maple syrup and salt and shake it until the glass gets cold and your espresso mixture is foamy.

If you're using a mason jar, you can use that as your cup and simply add your milk to the top, but if you're using a cocktail shaker, pour the mixture into a glass and top it with your milk. Watch as the milk cascades down the glass, swirling around the ice and slowly mixing with the foamy espresso.

Toasted Coconut Affogato

1 serving

A piping hot shot of espresso and a velvety helping of vanilla gelato—name a more iconic duo, I'll wait. The classic affogato is a standalone masterpiece, *but* this recipe tweaks the original one by using coconut gelato and adds toasted coconut on top. Coconut ice cream and gelato are a unique pair with espresso because of their sweet, creamy and uniquely tropical taste. In fact, coconut might be one of the few tropical fruits that pairs well with coffee. So, this rendition of the classic preserves the look of an affogato while keeping you on your toes as you dive into that first crunch of the toasted coconut shavings, the coolness of the gelato and the slurp of the espresso.

1 oz (30 ml) freshly brewed espresso

2 scoops of coconut ice cream or coconut gelato

Toasted coconut shavings, for garnish

Start by brewing your espresso. While it's brewing, put 2 generous scoops of the coconut ice cream into a glass. Pour your espresso over the ice cream, garnish with a few shavings of toasted coconut and enjoy.

Home Café Tip

Coconut shavings of the toasted variety can sometimes be hard to find in stores. If that's the case where you live, quickly toast your shavings by putting them in the oven on the broiler setting for 1 to 2 minutes, sometimes even less. And voilà, quick and easy toasted coconut shavings! Keep an eye on them, however, because they toast very quickly!

Wake Up, Lavender

1 serving

This recipe—I kid you not—came to me in a dream. I woke up suddenly in the middle of the night thinking about this book, and random flavors and pairings. Lavender and chocolate was one of them. I was like, "What?! Nooo." But I still wrote it down in my phone anyway. When I woke up, I looked at it again and thought the same thing. But that's what happens in movies, right? The person wakes up in a daze and absentmindedly scribbles something on a pad of paper. A few days later, I was testing some recipe ideas out, and this one turned out to be truly delicious!

Lavender Syrup

¼ cup (50 g) granulated sugar

1 tbsp (3 g) dried lavender petals

2 oz (60 ml) water

A few drops of purple food coloring (optional)

Mocha

2 oz (60 ml) chilled espresso

1 tbsp (15 ml) chocolate sauce or unsweetened cocoa powder

Ice

Lavender Syrup, to taste

8 oz (240 ml) milk of choice (I recommend 2% or any non-dairy alternative)

Dried lavender petals, for garnish

Start your drink prep by making your lavender syrup. In a small saucepan, combine the granulated sugar, dried lavender, water and food coloring (if using), and turn the heat to medium. Stir your mixture often until all the sugar dissolves, 2 to 3 minutes. Then, turn the heat to low and let it simmer for 5 to 7 minutes. The longer you let it simmer, the thicker it will be. Once it's done simmering, take your syrup off the heat, strain out the lavender petals and let it cool to room temperature. Store your syrup in an airtight container in the fridge for up to 1 week.

Begin your drink assembly by brewing your espresso shot. Once brewed, add the chocolate sauce to the shot and stir it until it has all dissolved. To a separate glass, add the ice, lavender syrup and milk. Last, top the lavender milk with your mocha shot. Create the layered effect by slowly pouring it over an ice cube or over the back of a spoon. Garnish it with some lavender petals.

Espresso Tónica

1 serving

The complex bitterness of the tonic water alongside the in-your-face espresso combine seamlessly to pique your interest. If you're skeptical, I get it. I was, too. If you've never had tonic before, it is bubbly and bitter with a touch of sweetness. While it can be an acquired taste, I implore you to take a chance on this sparkler . . . it might just persuade you to come over to Team Tonic.

2 oz (60 ml) chilled espresso

Ice

Lime slice, for garnish

6 oz (180 ml) tonic water

Begin by brewing your espresso a little bit ahead of time. After brewing, set it aside to cool or put it in the freezer for a few minutes to cool it down.

All that's left is to assemble your drink. Start by adding the ice to your glass. Before adding the tonic water, place the slice of lime on the wall of the glass, making sure the ice anchors it in place. This will ensure that you can see the lime instead of it getting lost in the darkness of the espresso. Next, add your tonic water to your glass, making sure to leave 1 to 2 inches (2.5 to 5 cm) at the top. Last, top the tonic with your chilled espresso shot, pouring slowly to create the layered effect.

Sparkling Espresso Lemonade

1 serving

This caffeinated lemonade will attack you on all fronts. Do you like bitter? Boom, espresso. You want something sweet and tart? Zing, lemonade! Are you in the mood for some bubbles? Bam, sparkling water. If you are unsure but curious about this trio, give it a try and see how you like it. Sometimes it's the drinks you never think will work that surprise you the most.

Sparkling Espresso

2 oz (60 ml) chilled espresso

Ice

8 oz (240 ml) sparkling water

Lemon slice, for garnish

Lemon Syrup

1 oz (30 ml) lemon juice

½ tsp lemon zest (optional)

1 tbsp (15 ml) sweetener of choice, or to taste (I recommend agave nectar)

Begin by brewing your espresso a little bit ahead of time. After brewing, set it aside to cool or put it in the freezer to cool off.

Now, you are going to make a super quick lemon syrup for your lemonade. To your glass, add the lemon juice, lemon zest (if using) and sweetener and stir well. You can start with the 1 tablespoon (15 ml) of sweetener specified above and add more/less depending on your taste. And there you have it—an instant lemon syrup!

Finish up your drink assembly by adding the ice to your glass, followed by your sparkling water, making sure to leave 1 to 2 inches (2.5 to 5 cm) of room at the top. Top the sparkling lemonade with the espresso shot and garnish your lemonade with a lemon slice.

Coffee, Coffee and *More Coffee*

Coffee is one of the most popular morning beverages in the world! It's our go-to when we need an extra jolt in the morning, the perfect accompaniment to any dessert and a favorite for anyone who uses it as a foundation for different milks, syrups and flavors. We've all been to a coffee shop at one point or another. They have classic recipes, holiday specials and their own signature drinks. I want you to think about the coffees you want to make in your home. The possibilities are truly endless!

The pages to come contain recipes to make in big batches and sips to enjoy solo. This chapter encompasses all things coffee that aren't espresso, from drip coffee to iced coffee to cold brew. Add the recipes to your home café menu, or let them be a jumping-off point for your own creativity. You'll see that a dessert you enjoyed as a child can be a delicious inspiration for a cold brew recipe, and that coffee doesn't just have to be brew, pour, sip.

Some of the most popular ways to make coffee are by way of electric drip makers, pour-over kits and French presses. The main difference between espresso and other types of coffee are the methods of brewing. The espresso method results in a small amount of highly concentrated coffee, whereas drip coffee, or what is known as "Americano"-style coffee, has a higher water content and is served in larger quantities.

Whichever way you like to drink your coffee, I hope this chapter inspires you to think about the ways you can spice up your morning cup of joe, even if it means adding a sprinkle of cinnamon or frothing up your milk.

The Classic Drip Coffee

1 serving

The classic drip coffee is an American staple. "Drip coffee" most commonly refers to coffee made in an electric coffee machine. In fact, if you grew up in America, your house most likely has a drip coffee machine. In my opinion, it is the easiest way to get caffeinated quickly early in the morning. Drip coffee is the perfect canvas for milk, creamers and your favorite sweeteners, but is delicate enough to drink on its own since it's water based. The coffee beans and the roast are up to you . . . but to be honest, it's hard to go wrong with a classic like this. Keep in mind that this recipe is a rough guide. You might like your coffee stronger or weaker than what's below, so have fun experimenting with what works best for you!

16 oz (480 ml) hot water

5 tbsp (20 g) coffee grounds of choice (I use medium roast)

Each coffee maker is a little different, but the concept is the same. When in doubt, refer to your machine's instructions, but here are the basic steps you'll use:

Start by adding the water to the reservoir of your coffee maker and place the coffee pot in its chamber. Next, add your coffee grounds to the filter in the basket of your coffee maker. Cover the basket, flip on the "on" switch and your coffee will be ready in no time.

The Classic Cold Brew

6 servings

Cold brew has become a rising favorite in America since the 2000s and has been a fast favorite in coffee shops since the 2010s. In the past 5 years, more and more people have been experimenting with making it at home, too. The great appeal of cold brew is that it requires minimal ingredients and tools, and it can be brewed while you sleep! It's also known to be less bitter and less acidic than other coffees because of the no-heat brewing method. If cold coffee is your thing, this recipe is great to have in your arsenal. The noteworthy feature about it is that you can make a big batch at the beginning of the week to enjoy whenever you need a little pick-me-up.

¾ cup (95 g) coarsely ground or whole coffee beans (medium or dark roast)

24 oz (720 ml) room temperature water (I recommend filtered)

If you're starting with whole beans, start by grinding them. You can choose to do it yourself if you have a coffee grinder, or you can grind them at the grocery store or ask your local coffee shop if they can help you out. Whichever way, make sure they are ground coarsely. If they are too fine, it can impact the taste and texture of your brew.

Once you have your coffee grounds, add them to a jar or container with a cover along with your filtered room temperature water. Stir your soon-to-be cold brew until all of the grounds are saturated with water and both ingredients are combined well. You can store the container at room temperature or in the fridge for anywhere from 12 to 18 hours. After much experimenting, I found that 14 to 16 hours is what I like best.

After the grounds have finished brewing, they are ready to be strained. You can strain them using a few different tools: a coffee filter (metal or paper), paper towels, a cheesecloth, a nut milk bag, a piece of cloth or a tea infuser.

Drink your cold brew as is or add ice, creamer, milk, syrups, sweeteners, etc.

Spiced Honey Coffee

1 serving

A cozy cuppa coffee is perfect for a rainy day . . . hell, any day for that matter. The spiced honey in this recipe is quick to put together, but its taste will make you feel so gourmet! The combo of the aromatic vanilla and nutmeg paired with the earthiness of the honey is a great complement to the bitterness of the coffee. While developing this recipe, I stood in front of my spice cabinet . . . just staring. Then, it hit me:

Vanilla + honey = comforting. Comfort food. Pie. Custard pie from Marie Callender's (a childhood staple). They used to sprinkle nutmeg on top of the custard pie, which was so good . . . I wish I had a piece right now . . . nutmeg! *Nutmeg!* *Nods head & smiles* And there you have it, a honey vanilla nutmeg coffee.

12 oz (360 ml) freshly brewed coffee
1 tbsp (15 ml) honey
A splash of vanilla extract or vanilla bean paste
A dash of ground nutmeg
Milk or creamer of choice, to taste (optional)

Begin by brewing your coffee. You can do this using the drip coffee method, pour-over method or by using a French press. While the coffee is brewing, make your quick honey vanilla nutmeg syrup. To your mug, add the honey, vanilla and ground nutmeg and stir them together until they are well combined.

Time to serve! Add your coffee to the spiced honey and mix them together until all of the honey dissolves. You can add some milk or cream if you'd like. Other than that, you are good to go.

Foamy Spiced Maple Café

1 serving

Are you looking for an easy yet flavorful addition to your morning coffee? Look no further than this spiced maple coffee. It tastes like a big stack of French toast with a generous pouring of maple syrup on top. This coffee uses the warm spices of cinnamon and cloves to deepen the coziness of the maple syrup. This recipe is like a hug in a cup. So, prepare your blanket fort, put on your fuzzy socks and enjoy this snuggly sip.

12 oz (360 ml) hot coffee
1 tbsp (15 ml) maple syrup
A dash of ground cloves
A dash of ground cinnamon, plus more for garnish
Milk or creamer of choice, to taste

Begin by brewing your coffee. You can do this using the drip coffee method, pour-over method or by using a French press. While your coffee is brewing, make your spiced maple foam. Add the maple syrup, cloves, cinnamon and milk to a cup or to a standing milk frother, and froth them together until the mixture is well combined and foamy, 30 to 45 seconds.

Last, pour the coffee into your mug, leaving 1 to 2 inches (2.5 to 5 cm) of room at the top, and then pour the spiced maple foam into your mug until it reaches the top. Garnish it with a sprinkle of ground cinnamon.

Honeycomb Coffee

1 serving

Honeycomb candy induces an instant smile! If you've never had honeycomb candy or sponge candy, it's not necessarily meant to mimic the taste of an actual piece of honeycomb, but it has a toasty caramel flavor and crunchy texture and looks similar to a real honeycomb. It's also surprisingly easy to make with only two ingredients: sugar and baking soda. When assembling your drink, you can even pour your milk over your honeycomb. The moisture of the milk will slowly dissolve the sugar in the honeycomb; it's like being a kid in a coffee shop.

¼ cup (50 g) granulated sugar
1 tsp baking soda
12 oz (360 ml) freshly brewed coffee
Milk or creamer of choice, to taste (optional)

Begin your drink prep by making the honeycomb. First, lay out a sheet of parchment paper on a flat surface. You'll be pouring your honeycomb on this to prevent it from sticking to other surfaces. Add the granulated sugar to a small pan on medium heat. After a few minutes, the sugar will slowly start to melt. Stir the sugar every so often to prevent it from burning. Sugar clumps will start to develop, but as long as you stir your mixture periodically, the clumps will dissolve. It will take about 10 minutes for the sugar to melt completely and become an amber brown color.

(continued)

Honeycomb Coffee *(continued)*

Take your caramel off the heat and add in your baking soda. This is where you need to be a little quick. Your mixture will immediately start doubling in size and turn a creamy caramel color. Using a silicone spatula or flexible spoon of some sort, stir the mixture to combine the caramel and baking soda. Don't stir it too much or else the airiness will deflate. When the mixture has just come together, pour it onto your parchment paper. I recommend pouring it in a big mound. The taller the honeycomb, the more details you'll see inside once you break it open. Let the honeycomb cool for at least 10 minutes. When serving, break apart your honeycomb by lifting it roughly 5 inches (13 cm) off the parchment and letting it fall. This will cause the honeycomb to crack, revealing an intricate, honeycomb-like pattern inside. Store it covered in a dry, cool place or eat it right away.

Start your drink assembly by brewing your coffee. Do this using the drip coffee method, pour-over method or by using a French press. Once brewed, pour the coffee into your mug of choice, then anchor a piece of honeycomb over the top of your mug. And if you like, top off your coffee with some milk or creamer of choice.

Salty Maple Cold Brew Granita

1 serving

I love this four-ingredient Salty Maple Cold Brew Granita. Although the recipe sounds like it's kind of complicated with the freezing and whipping that's involved, it's actually very simple. The trio of cold brew, maple syrup and sea salt make for a well-rounded experience that's cooling and creamy. This is the perfect dessert to serve to coffee-loving friends and family at any time of the year, but especially summer!

8 oz (240 ml) The Classic Cold Brew (page 55)
4 tbsp (60 ml) maple syrup, divided, plus more for garnish
Sea salt, plus more for garnish
1 oz (30 ml) heavy cream

Start by making your cold brew granita. First, you will want to have some cold brew on hand. See The Classic Cold Brew recipe (page 55) or use your favorite store-bought brew. Pour the cold brew, 2 tablespoons (30 ml) of maple syrup and a small pinch of salt in a metal pan or bowl, stir until it's combined and place it in the freezer for 1 hour.

After the hour is up, take your cold brew out of the freezer and scrape it with a fork, crushing all the solid, frozen pieces until they become snow-like. Your mixture will still have a mostly liquid consistency after the first scrape. Place your soon-to-be granita back into the freezer and continue to scrape it every 15 to 20 minutes until all of the coffee has frozen completely. Be sure to set aside 2 hours in total, as you will need to scrape your granita over the course of the next hour to get the perfect consistency. You'll know it's ready when it looks like coffee snow! I would suggest enjoying it right when it's ready, but you can keep it in the freezer for up to 5 days, mixing and scraping it once a day or so.

(continued)

Salty Maple Cold Brew Granita *(continued)*

Now, it's time to make the salty maple whipped cream. In a small bowl, add the remaining 2 tablespoons (30 ml) of maple syrup, heavy cream and a generous pinch of sea salt. Before whisking, taste test your cream and add more maple syrup or salt as desired. Then, whisk the ingredients together until it has semi-stiff peaks. You'll know your whipped cream is ready when you are able to scoop it and it's able to keep its shape. It should take 5 to 10 minutes. Last, scoop some of the cold brew granita into a glass and top it with a generous scoop of the salty maple whipped cream, an extra drizzle of maple syrup and an extra pinch of salt!

Home Café Tip

Chill the bowl (preferably metal) that you plan to use for whipping your cream in the freezer for 5 to 10 minutes beforehand. The coldness of the bowl will help the cream whip faster and chill it perfectly to pair with your granita. This step is not mandatory, but a simple way to instantly elevate your home café game and whipping experience.

Campfire Iced Coffee

1 serving

This @ac_homecafé classic is an absolute must-try and my *all-time* favorite. A while back, way before I started drinking coffee, my mom bought a latte with toasted marshmallow syrup in it from a random coffee shop and wanted to have some to enjoy at home. She looked all over town (oftentimes dragging me with her) to find this dang toasted marshmallow syrup. After a couple months, we finally found it at World Market! I knew when I started developing recipes for my home café that I needed to create an at-home version of toasted marshmallow syrup for my mom, and it soon became a favorite of mine as well.

Toasted Marshmallow Syrup

10 mini toasted marshmallows or 2 jumbo toasted marshmallows

¼ cup (50 g) granulated sugar

2 oz (60 ml) water

A tiny splash of vanilla extract

Iced Coffee

Toasted Marshmallow Syrup, to taste

Ice

10 oz (300 ml) chilled coffee

Milk or creamer of choice, to taste

Toasted marshmallows, for garnish (optional)

Begin your drink prep by making your toasted marshmallow syrup. First, toast your marshmallows. Ideally, an open-fire source like a bonfire is best for this! But you can also use a gas stove, match or lighter. Don't let the marshmallows burn for too long to avoid picking up any chemicals from these sources. Next, to a small saucepan over medium heat, add your toasted marshmallows, sugar, water and vanilla extract. Stir the mixture often until all of the sugar and marshmallows dissolve. You might have to break up the pieces of marshmallow with your spoon or spatula as they melt. You'll know it's time to take your syrup off the heat when there are no more sugar crystals, and the white pieces of marshmallow are gone, usually 3 to 5 minutes. Take the syrup off the heat, let it cool to room temperature and strain out the leftover burnt marshmallow pieces. You can store it in an airtight container in the fridge for up to 1 week.

Assemble your drink by adding the syrup, ice and coffee to your glass. Top off the coffee with your milk or creamer and watch closely as it swirls down the walls of your glass . . . it's quite mesmerizing. And if you're feeling fancy, garnish it with a couple more toasted marshmallows.

Shaken White Mocha Iced Coffee

1 serving

This is a great beverage for when you are craving something a bit on the sweet side. I use store-bought white mocha sauce—there are lots of different options, so don't be afraid to sample them all to find what you like. The creamy, vanilla-esque flavors of the white mocha sauce are the perfect complement to the bite of the coffee. Shaking everything up will emulsify the white mocha sauce and make it perfectly velvety. Just because you're enjoying your coffee at home doesn't mean you can't shake it up a bit!

2 tbsp (30 ml) white mocha sauce, plus more for garnish

Ice

8 oz (240 ml) chilled coffee

Milk or creamer of choice, to taste

In your mason jar or cocktail shaker, combine the white mocha sauce, ice and chilled coffee. Shake it up until all of the white mocha has dissolved, 15 to 20 seconds, or until your arm gets tired!

If you're shaking it in a mason jar, you can keep it in there for less cleanup and so you can see the beautiful auburn color turn into a creamy beige as the mocha sauce disperses. Finish your drink off with a splash of milk or creamer and a drizzle of white mocha sauce and enjoy!

Ube Coffee Float

1 serving

Have you tried ube? Ube, pronounced "ooo-beh," is a purple yam popular in the Philippines and other parts of Asia. It is an instant showstopper because of its natural purple color and slightly sweet and nutty taste. You wouldn't usually expect for a yam to be this versatile, right? Ube not only tastes great as an ice cream, but it also flavors jam (ube halaya), breads, cakes, mochi . . . the list is endless. This recipe uses ube in its ice cream form, which adds an extra layer of creaminess to the classic iced coffee taste. If your local grocery store doesn't stock ube ice cream, you can find it at almost any Asian market in your area, like 99 Ranch Market, Seafood City and 168 Market.

Ice (optional)
10 oz (300 ml) chilled coffee
Milk or creamer of choice, to taste
1 generous scoop of ube ice cream

This one is super quick! Head straight to assembly by adding your ice (if using), chilled coffee and milk or creamer to your glass. Then, top off your iced coffee with a generous scoop of ube ice cream.

Cheese Foam Iced Coffee

1 serving

Cheese foam! I hope I didn't lose you just yet because cheese foam is so much more nuanced and compelling than you might think. Yeah, I just used "compelling" to describe a whipped topping. Am I reaching? Maybe, but I will remain reaching with a cheese foam iced coffee in hand. Inspired by the cheese foam that commonly tops green and black teas in boba shops, this recipe uses that same popular cheese foam on top of everyone's favorite: iced coffee. If you're skeptical, I get it. It's cheese on coffee! But I urge you to try this sweet and slightly tart, creamy treat.

Cheese Foam

1 tbsp (15 g) cream cheese

1 tbsp (15 g) sweetener of choice, or to taste (I recommend agave or granulated sugar)

1 oz (30 ml) heavy cream

½ oz (15 ml) milk of choice (I recommend 2% or any non-dairy alternative)

Coffee

Ice

10 oz (300 ml) chilled coffee

Cheese Foam, to taste

Begin by making your cheese foam. In a small bowl or cup, add your cream cheese and sweetener. I recommend stirring them together until combined to help soften the cream cheese. Once the two are combined and semi-smooth, add your heavy cream and milk and whisk or froth them until your cream is fluffy and light. It should take about 5 minutes.

For the drink assembly, add the ice and coffee to your glass, making sure to leave approximately 2 inches (5 cm) on top. Last, top your coffee off with your cheese foam. Once it's poured, watch as the foam gently cascades down the side of the glass. Did you really have an iced coffee if you didn't take a picture of it?

Cookies 'n' Cream Coffee

1 serving

Another @ac_homecafé classic, this cookies 'n' cream iced coffee made its debut on Instagram in July 2020, and it is an immediate "double sipper." In other words, it's one of those coffees where you take that first taste to see what's going on and immediately take another because it's so good. This is my second favorite coffee recipe of all time behind the Campfire Iced Coffee (page 66). This drink is a fantasy come to life. The light and airy whipped cream combined with the crème sandwich crumbles is a treat in itself, but it's taken to a new level when paired with the iced coffee! My favorite part of enjoying this drink is munching on the little chocolate cookie pieces along the way.

2–3 crème sandwich cookies or Oreos, plus more for garnish

1 oz (30 ml) heavy cream

Ice

10 oz (300 ml) chilled coffee

Begin by making your cookies 'n' cream . . . cream. You can crush the cookies using the bottom of a cup, cut them up with a knife or put them in a baggy and whack them on the counter. Whichever method you choose, make sure that there are no *really* big chunks. You're going to be drinking this, after all. Next, in a small bowl, whip the heavy cream with a handheld frother or whisk. It should take 3 to 5 minutes with a normal whisk and about 1 minute with a handheld frother to get to the perfect foamy consistency. Be careful to not whip it for too long because it may become hard to pour. Once your cream is whipped, add in the small cookie pieces and stir until they are well incorporated. The cream should have a black-and-white speckled look. I'm getting thirsty just thinking about it!

Now it's time to assemble—add the ice and coffee to your glass, then top it off with the cookies 'n' cream, cream.

Gingerbread Cold Brew

1 serving

Gingerbread people, gingerbread houses, ginger snap cookies . . . what do all of these treats have in common? That delectable combo of ginger, warming spices and the molasses-y crunch of the brown sugar. It doesn't get much better than that. The three main components of this gingery cold brew are the gingerbread syrup, cold brew and milk. If you want to get a little fancy, you can combine the syrup and milk in a separate cup and froth those together to create a gingerbread cold foam.

Gingerbread Syrup

2 oz (60 ml) water

¼ cup (50 g) brown sugar

A dash of ground ginger

A dash of ground cinnamon

A dash of ground nutmeg

A dash of ground cloves

Gingerbread Cold Brew

10 oz (300 ml) The Classic Cold Brew (page 55)

Ice

Gingerbread Syrup, to taste

Milk or creamer of choice, to taste (optional)

You will want to have some cold brew on hand for this recipe. See The Classic Cold Brew recipe (page 55) or use your favorite store-bought cold brew.

Begin your drink prep by making your gingerbread syrup. In a small saucepan, add the water, brown sugar, ginger, cinnamon, nutmeg and cloves and warm over medium heat. Stir it occasionally until the sugar dissolves and the spices are well combined. Once all of the sugar has dissolved, turn the heat down to low and let your syrup simmer for 5 to 7 minutes, stirring it every so often. This will help your syrup thicken. After you let it simmer, take it off the heat and let it cool to room temperature. Store your syrup in an airtight container in the fridge for up to 1 week.

Let's assemble! Add the ice, gingerbread syrup and cold brew to your glass. Finish your drink off by adding some milk or creamer, or leave it black if you prefer.

Honey Lavender Cold Brew

1 serving

The aroma of this beverage is heavenly. This cold brew recipe was inspired by the famous pairing of honey and lavender. I can just imagine you enjoying this glass of cold brew while basking in a sunny meadow surrounded by blooming lavender flowers. While we can't enjoy our coffee in sunny meadows every day, I can assure you that this drink will help you get there. If you love the unique aroma of lavender, this drink is a must-try!

Lavender Honey Syrup

2 oz (60 ml) honey

2 oz (60 ml) water

1 tbsp (3 g) dried lavender petals

A few drops of purple food coloring (optional)

Cold Brew

Ice

Lavender Honey Syrup, to taste

10 oz (300 ml) The Classic Cold Brew (page 55)

Milk or creamer of choice, to taste (optional)

Begin your drink prep by making the lavender honey syrup. In a small saucepan over medium heat, combine the honey, water, dried lavender and food coloring (if using). Stir your soon-to-be syrup occasionally until all of the honey dissolves. Then, turn the heat down to low and let your syrup simmer for 5 to 7 minutes to help it thicken. When it's done simmering, take it off the heat, strain out the lavender petals and let it cool to room temperature. Store your syrup in an airtight container in the fridge for up to 2 weeks.

Add your ice, lavender honey syrup and cold brew to your glass of choice. This cold brew is great with or without milk or creamer, so take a sip, see what you prefer and enjoy!

Be Bold Brew

1 serving

The coolness of the cold brew will tame the warmth of the chocolate milk in this spicy chocolate concoction. One of my biggest sources of inspiration is putting a caffeinated twist on childhood favorites. This drink takes the newer, popular cold brew and bridges a gap with a staple in almost every Mexican household: Abuelita chocolate. The dashes of chili and ground cinnamon make for an interesting contrast between the ice and chocolatey spiced milk. Want to be bold? Try this brew!

Ice
10 oz (300 ml) The Classic Cold Brew (page 55)
1 oz (30 ml) milk or creamer of choice
2 tbsp (30 ml) chocolate sauce, plus more for garnish
A dash of ground cinnamon
A dash of chili powder
A pinch of salt

Begin your drink assembly by adding the ice and cold brew to your glass. In another cup, combine your milk, chocolate sauce, ground cinnamon, chili powder and salt. Mix the ingredients together until they are well combined. Pour the spiced chocolate milk "shot" over your cold brew and garnish it with a generous squeeze of chocolate sauce!

Home Café Tip

There are many different types of chocolate sauce options to choose from when building your own home café. My favorite store-bought options are Torani and Ghirardelli milk and dark chocolate sauces, which can be found in almost any grocery store near you.

More Matcha *Please*

Matcha: The bright green drink you've seen on TV, Instagram and TikTok. You can enjoy it hot or cold, with ice or without, creamy or with some sort of fruity element. But what is it? Matcha is made by grinding green tea leaves into a fine grit or powder, then whisking the powder into hot water. With rich origins in China and Japan, matcha has become a fast favorite in the U.S. because of its high caffeine content. This comes from consuming the whole tea leaf instead of it being steeped like most other green tea blends. It is thicker, creamier and has a more natural sweetness than other green teas.

Matcha powder comes in a few different types or grades. Ceremonial-grade matcha is the most popular and is known worldwide as the highest grade of matcha there is. In addition to being more expensive at around $20 per 1½ ounces (42 g), it has a vibrant green color that gives any beverage a rich, green tea taste with an extra umph of caffeine. The second most readily available is culinary-grade matcha. This grade possesses a less vivid color but is the most affordable form of matcha at around $9 per 1½ ounces (42 g). For both ceremonial and culinary grade, 1½ ounces (42 g) may sound miniscule, but it usually lasts 4 to 6 months if you drink matcha once or twice a week.

As mentioned in the Tea Tools section (page 14), matcha is traditionally prepared by using a matcha whisk, matcha powder, a bowl and water (hot or room temperature). Although it's possible to mix matcha with a frother or spoon, there is nothing like a matcha whisk. As you'll see, the easiest way to prepare matcha is to add the ingredients to your bowl and whisk them together in a "W" shape. This ensures that all of the matcha clumps are being broken down and will dissolve seamlessly into your drink.

The recipes in this chapter are full of lots of different flavors—some are classic, some are new. If matcha is a new flavor for you, the drinks to come will let you mingle with that first taste and get you acclimated with its depth. If you're already a matcha lover, I can't wait for you to explore the different layers it has to offer. From creamy matcha latte creations to the light, bubbly and citrusy drinks, you'll be saying, "More matcha, please!"

Matcha-Misù Tea Latte

1 serving

A variation of a variation, this matcha-misù latte offers the decadence of a tiramisù latte but replaces the robust flavor of espresso with matcha's aromatic notes. The matcha powder paired with the creamy mascarpone whipped topping makes for an instant "treat yo-self" moment. You can even dip some ladyfingers in this tea latte for a deconstructed matcha-misù experience. I hope you enjoy this drinkable dessert!

8 oz (240 ml) milk of choice (I recommend oat)
1 tbsp (18 g) mascarpone cheese
1–2 tsp (10–20 ml) sweetener of choice (I recommend agave)
2 oz (60 ml) heavy cream
1½ tsp (4 g) matcha powder, plus more for garnish
1 oz (30 ml) hot water

Start by heating up your milk. You can do this with a steamer, on the stove over medium-high heat until it comes to a light boil or you can warm it up in the microwave for 2 minutes. While the milk is heating, in a small bowl, begin making your mascarpone cream by combining your mascarpone cheese and sweetener and mixing these two ingredients together until the mascarpone softens slightly. Because mascarpone is a fairly thick cheese, this step will ensure that it's easily mixable during the whipping process. To the mascarpone and sweetener, add the heavy cream and whip it until it is thick and pourable, but not so much that it becomes whipped cream.

Begin making the matcha shot by combining your matcha powder with the hot water in a cup or bowl. You can combine them with a matcha whisk or frother until all of the matcha clumps have dissolved. Make sure to save a little extra matcha powder to sprinkle on top at the end.

In your mug, combine the steamed milk and matcha shot to make a bright, creamy green color. Top your matcha latte mixture with your mascarpone cream and sprinkle with a generous dusting of matcha powder.

Spiced Maple Matcha

1 serving

You will want to snuggle up on the couch in a mound of blankets with this tea latte. I say this because that's exactly what I did after testing out this drink. Maple is such an underrated drink sweetener, so if you have yet to try it, I would highly recommend it. The maple syrup paired with cinnamon and nutmeg immediately transport you to a dreamy matcha wonderland. Feel free to garnish this tea latte with a sprinkle of cinnamon or nutmeg for some extra coziness.

6 oz (180 ml) milk of choice (I recommend oat or almond)
1 tsp matcha powder
2 oz (60 ml) hot water
2 tbsp (30 ml) maple syrup, or to taste
A dash of ground cinnamon, plus more for garnish
A dash of ground nutmeg, plus more for garnish

Begin by heating up your milk. You can do this with a steamer, on the stove over medium-high heat until it comes to a light boil or you can warm it up in the microwave for 2 minutes. In the meantime, start to make your matcha shot. To do this, combine your matcha powder and water in a glass, and whisk or froth them together until all the matcha clumps dissolve.

In your mug, combine your maple syrup, cinnamon, nutmeg and steamed milk, and froth until they are all combined. I like my tea lattes extra foamy, but the beauty of a home café is that you can make your drink how *you* like!

Once combined, add your matcha shot to the spiced maple milk. To create the layered effect, pour your matcha shot *very* slowly into your milk and garnish it with some more ground cinnamon or ground nutmeg.

Home Café Tip

The ombré effect of different colors is so satisfying, especially in matcha drinks. An easy way to get that layered look is to pour your matcha shot over the back of a spoon. This will break the heavy stream of the matcha and create a shadow from white to light green . . . so satisfying!

La Vie En Rose Latte

1 serving

I took one sip of this tea latte and could have sworn that birds started chirping and the sun started shining a little bit brighter. This is one of my personal favorite matcha drinks! Since matcha has a bright, vegetal quality, the floral notes of the vanilla rose syrup make for a great pairing. If you're having reservations about this drink, I get it. Matcha can be somewhat of an acquired taste and rose can be too aromatic if overused, *but* the thread that holds these flavors together is the vanilla. Its familiar aroma helps your palate find common ground between the matcha and the rose.

Vanilla Rose Syrup

½ cup (100 g) granulated sugar

4 oz (120 ml) water

A tiny splash of vanilla extract

1½ oz (45 ml) rose water or 3 tbsp (15 g) dried rose petals

A few drops of red food coloring or beetroot powder (optional)

Tea Latte

6 oz (180 ml) milk of choice (I recommend oat or pistachio)

1 tsp matcha powder

2 oz (60 ml) hot water

Vanilla Rose Syrup, to taste

Dried rose petals, for garnish

Start your drink prep by making your vanilla rose syrup. In a small saucepan, combine your granulated sugar, water, vanilla, rose water and red food coloring (if using). Heat on medium until all of the sugar has dissolved, then turn the heat down to low and let your syrup simmer for 5 to 7 minutes. This will thicken the syrup a little more. Take your syrup off the heat and strain out the rose petals, if you used them. Let it cool to room temperature and pour it into an airtight container. Store it in an airtight container in the fridge for up to 2 weeks.

To make your tea latte, begin by heating up your milk. You can do this with a steamer, on the stove over medium-high heat until it comes to a light boil or you can warm it up in the microwave for 2 minutes. While that's heating up, add your matcha powder and water to a bowl and whisk or froth until all of the matcha clumps have dissolved. Next, add your vanilla rose syrup to your mug along with your steamed milk. If you chose to add food coloring, your milk should be a blush-pink color. Last, slowly pour your matcha shot over the back of a spoon into the mug to create a layered effect. Finish by sprinkling a few dried rose petals over the top of your latte.

Double Chocolate Matcha Float

1 serving

Matcha drinks don't just have to be matcha powder, water and milk. The great thing about matcha rising in popularity in the U.S. is that we are getting easier access to matcha *everything*! Cakes, candies, breads, cookies—you name it. So, why not substitute a matcha shot for a scoop of matcha ice cream? That's exactly what you'll do with this simple and delicious recipe. It's a little on the sweet side, but you can adjust the sweetness by adding or holding back on the amount of chocolate sauce that you use.

1 tbsp (15 ml) white chocolate sauce

6 oz (180 ml) milk of choice (I recommend 2% or any non-dairy alternative)

1 tbsp (15 ml) chocolate sauce

Ice

1 scoop of matcha ice cream

Begin by making your white chocolate milk. In a cup, combine your white chocolate sauce with your milk, and stir it until all of the sauce is incorporated.

Start constructing your float by adding your chocolate sauce to your glass. The easiest way to do this is to hold your glass in one hand and the chocolate sauce in the other. Pour it in around the top inner rim of your glass and gravity will do the rest, making the chocolate sauce cascade down the sides of your glass. Then you can add your ice and white chocolate milk. Top off your drink with a generous scoop of matcha ice cream and enjoy!

Mixed Berry Bubbly Matcha

1 serving

This matcha sparkler will hit your palate with the tingle of the sparkling water, subtlety of the matcha and sweetness of mixed berry goodness. When I was little, my cousins and I used to make potions out of random ingredients from the pantry. This drink is an ode to those days, except that this one is actually drinkable. The combination of the sparkling water, matcha and fruitiness was purely experimental at first, but there is something so fun about discovering these delicious new flavors by chance.

1 tsp matcha powder
2 oz (60 ml) room temperature water
4–5 blackberries, plus more for garnish
2–3 diced strawberries, plus more for garnish
1 tsp sweetener of choice, or to taste (I recommend agave)
Ice
8 oz (240 ml) sparkling water

Start by preparing your matcha shot. In a small bowl, combine the matcha powder and water and mix with your matcha whisk or frother until there are no more matcha clumps left. Set this aside for later.

To your glass, add your blackberries, strawberries and sweetener of choice. Muddle these ingredients together until the berries are crushed and everything is well combined. Add ice on top of your mixed berry mixture and top it with sparkling water, leaving 1 to 2 inches (2.5 to 5 cm) of room at the top. Pour your matcha over the top of your drink and watch as the clear sparkling water turns a bright green color. Finish it by garnishing with extra berries.

Home Café Tip

The blackberries, strawberries and sweetener in this recipe can be substituted with mixed berry jam for a quick shortcut! I do enjoy homemaking my berry syrup, but there is something so quick and easy about using jam that I just can't ignore, especially on busy days. Do what's doable for you!

The Lemongrass Lady

1 serving

The unique flavors of this lemongrass matcha iced tea will awaken your palate in ways you never thought possible. Lemongrass is more commonly used in savory dishes like curries, soups and marinades, but this recipe takes lemongrass and makes it the star of the show. Its lemony, herbaceous flavor paired with the ceremonial matcha is certainly an eye-opener after your first sip. This drink is best enjoyed cold, but it is great as a hot cuppa tea too!

Lemongrass Tea

2–3 lemongrass stalks with leaves

10 oz (300 ml) water

Iced Tea

1 tsp matcha powder

2 oz (60 ml) room temperature water

Ice

8 oz (240 ml) Lemongrass Tea

1 tsp sweetener of choice, or to taste (I recommend agave)

Lemongrass stalk or lemon slice, for garnish

Begin your drink prep by making your lemongrass tea. Roughly chop the lemongrass stalks and add them to a medium pot of water on medium heat. Bring the mixture to a boil and then lower it to medium-low heat for an additional 5 minutes. Strain the stalks out and let your tea cool until it reaches room temperature. You can store it in the fridge in an airtight container for 3 to 4 days.

In a small bowl, make your matcha shot by combining your matcha powder and water, whisking until all the matcha clumps have dissolved. To your glass, add your ice, matcha shot, lemongrass tea and sweetener of choice. Last, garnish it with a lemongrass stalk for an instant stirrer, or a lemon slice.

Icy Guava Matcha

1 serving

Guava is one of my forever favorites. Yes, *forever*! Something just awakens inside me when I smell guava. I'm positive that it has something to do with my Pacific Islander and South American roots. Some of my fondest memories involve guava, like smelling the guava trees in my great-grandpa's backyard when I'd go visit and enjoying a glass of POG (Passion Orange Guava) when visiting Hawaii. If you've never had guava before, it kind of tastes like a combination of a lemon, a pear and a strawberry. And guava nectar is even tastier! You can find guava nectar, which is basically guava juice, online or at your local grocery store. This slush is citrusy, vibrant and perfectly balanced by the bitterness of the matcha shot.

1 tsp matcha powder

2 oz (60 ml) room temperature water

6 oz (180 ml) guava nectar

1 oz (30 ml) lime juice

¾ cup (170 g) ice

Lime slice, for garnish

Begin by making your matcha shot. To do this, combine your matcha powder and water in a small bowl and whisk or froth until all matcha clumps have completely dissolved. Set this aside for later.

In a blender, combine the guava nectar, lime juice and ice and blend until your mixture is smooth. Next, pour your guava lime mixture into your glass of choice and top it with the matcha shot by slowly pouring it over the icy guava goodness. Garnish it with a lime slice and enjoy!

Home Café Tip

Want to make a lime flower like the one in the picture? I learned this super easy trick from @onedrinkaday on Instagram. To do this, take a whole lime and make 5 to 6 tiny "V"-shaped slits on the outside. Remove the lime segments that you cut out and slice your lime as usual. Once sliced, your flower design will be revealed.

Sparkling Matcha Lemonade

1 serving

There's nothing like sitting outside on a sunny day enjoying a tall, refreshing glass of lemonade. We are swapping out black tea for matcha in a twist on the beloved Arnold Palmer half & half iced tea lemonade. This lemonade is unique in that it's sweetened by the matcha syrup and uses sparkling water instead of still water. If you're a matcha skeptic, the flavors in this sparkling lemonade will make you a convert.

Matcha Syrup

2 oz (60 ml) room temperature water

1 tsp matcha powder

¼ cup (50 g) granulated sugar

Lemonade

2 tbsp (30 ml) Matcha Syrup

Ice

8 oz (240 ml) sparkling water

1 oz (30 ml) lemon juice

Lemon slices, for garnish

Start your drink preparation by making the matcha syrup. To a small saucepan, add the water and matcha powder and whisk or froth until all of the matcha clumps have dissolved. To the matcha mixture, add the granulated sugar. Heat the ingredients on medium until the matcha is fully combined and the sugar is dissolved, stirring often. Once all the sugar has dissolved, turn the heat down to low and let the syrup simmer for 5 to 7 minutes. The thicker you want your syrup to be, the longer you can let it simmer. Take the syrup off the heat, let it cool completely and store it in the fridge in an airtight container for up to 1 week.

Start assembling your drink by adding your matcha syrup to your glass. Then, add the ice followed by your favorite sparkling water and lemon juice. Finally, garnish with fresh lemon slices for that Insta-worthy pic!

Home Café Tip

There's nothing like a good layering effect for a post-able drink picture on your socials. Pouring in the matcha syrup before the rest of the ingredients will create the instant layered look without having to pour slowly or use special tools!

The Bright Side

1 serving

I often buy a bag of tangerines with high hopes . . . hopes for me to eat two or three a day and to finish a whole bag without any of them going bad. This has yet to happen in my adult life. In fact, my family often delivers bags of citrus on my doorstep because they, too, face the same problem. I've discovered, however, that juicing can be a great solution. Do you have some extra tangerines that are about to go bad? Look on the bright side and try this recipe. And while you're at it, add in some matcha and honey and you're already halfway to making this citrusy, aromatic concoction.

8 oz (240 ml) tangerine juice (about 5–6 tangerines)

1 tsp matcha powder

2 oz (60 ml) room temperature water

2 tsp (10 ml) honey

Ice

Tangerine slice, for garnish

Begin your drink preparation by juicing your tangerines. Don't forget to save a tangerine slice for garnish! Once the tangerines are juiced, in a small bowl, prepare your matcha by combining matcha powder with your water and whisking or frothing it until all of the matcha clumps have dissolved.

To your glass, add the honey and tangerine juice and mix it until the honey is completely dissolved. To this mixture, add your ice and matcha shot. If you want to create that layered effect, pour your matcha over the back of a spoon *very* slowly, or pour it over the top of an ice cube to break its fall. Garnish your beautiful beverage with a tangerine slice and enjoy!

Hey, *Hot-Tea*

It's been decided . . . hotties love hot tea. From Ceylon and Assam to English and Irish, this chapter embraces all things black tea, with fresh takes on the classic hot cuppa tea, recipes for tea lattes and even tea spritzers.

All kinds of tea (but black tea in particular) have been a very special part of my life and have always been a popular beverage in my house. It's been a comfort after a bad day, a remedy for a cold and a drink associated with happy memories. My dad's favorite drink of all time was a trenta iced black tea from Starbucks, so much so that learning how to make his order was part of the training curriculum at his local Starbucks! Much like him, black tea is a forever favorite, with my go-to being Earl Grey or Constant Comment. Growing up, I would go to my grandparents' house after school and my Grama and I would have afternoon tea parties with little cookies or treats and have tea served from her collection of vintage teapots and teacups. We had Bigelow's Constant Comment almost every single day. To this day, the mere smell of that tea is an instant transport to those special times with my Grama and is one of the main reasons why drinks as a whole are so special to me. They bring people together. They are something to share with loved ones or a way to break the ice with people you are just getting to know.

Black teas are one of the most essential components of a home café because they offer a solid foundation for other flavors and preparations. They are strong enough to handle milks and creams while grounding the bolder flavors of syrups and citrus. The recipes to come are inspired by classic teas with modern twists using herbs, fruity elements and different milky accompaniments that are reminiscent of high tea and boba shop specialties. So, tea kettles on, and pinkies out!

Blueberry Lavender Tea Latte

1 serving

Alright, hot-teas, let's talk about this dreamy cuppa Earl Grey. Loosely based on the London Fog Tea Latte, the addition of blueberry to the already floral lavender will give you that eye-opening first sip. You might be thinking, fruit, milk *and* tea? Trust me, you've got to try this! This recipe requires homemaking the blueberry lavender syrup, but not to worry, I have a few tips and tricks on how to dramatically cut down your prep and cleanup time. This is a tea latte fit for a royal . . . that's you!

Blueberry Lavender Syrup

¼ cup (40 g) frozen blueberries

1 tsp dried lavender petals

2 oz (60 ml) water

¼ cup (50 g) granulated sugar

Tea Latte

2 oz (60 ml) hot water

2 Earl Grey tea bags or 2 tbsp (10 g) Earl Grey tea leaves

10 oz (300 ml) milk of choice (I recommend oat or almond)

Blueberry Lavender Syrup, to taste

Dried lavender petals, for garnish

Begin by making your blueberry lavender syrup. You can do this one of two ways:

Microwave Method: In a microwaveable bowl or cup, add your blueberries, lavender and water and microwave on high for 2 minutes. Your blueberries should look plump and your mixture should have steam coming off the top when it comes out of the microwave. To your mixture, add your sugar and stir until all of it has dissolved. While you're stirring, you can mash the blueberries to release their color and flavor even more. Once all the sugar has dissolved, strain out the blueberry and lavender bits, let your syrup cool and store it in an airtight container in the fridge for up to 1 week.

(continued)

Blueberry Lavender Tea Latte *(continued)*

Stovetop Method: To a small saucepan over medium heat, add the blueberries, lavender, water and sugar. Stir your mixture occasionally until all the sugar has dissolved. Then, turn your heat to low and let your syrup simmer for 5 to 7 minutes. Take the syrup off the heat, strain out the blueberry and lavender bits and let it cool. You can store your syrup in the fridge in an airtight container for up to 1 week.

Start constructing your drink by brewing your tea. In a cup, combine the hot water and Earl Grey tea and let it steep until it reaches your desired strength. While your tea is steeping, you can heat up and froth your milk. Heat up your milk in a small pot on the stove over medium-high heat until it reaches a light boil (about 5 minutes), or microwave it for 2 minutes. You can choose to froth your milk or leave it as is. Then, add the blueberry lavender syrup and steamed milk to your mug and top it off with your Earl Grey tea shot. Garnish your latte with some dried lavender and enjoy!

Honey, Do You Like Sesame?

1 serving

Black sesame seeds aren't just for everything bagels anymore. Some of my favorite black sesame desserts growing up were (and still are) fried sesame balls filled with sweet red bean, sesame mochi soup and black sesame ice cream. This tea latte takes the unique toasted and nutty-tasting black sesame seeds and transforms them into a tea topper fit for current fans of sesame desserts and anyone curious about new flavors. This recipe calls for either crushed black sesame seeds or black sesame powder. Black sesame seeds can sometimes be hard to find in stores, but you can find them online at Weee!, Yummy Bazaar or Amazon.

1 tbsp (10 g) crushed black sesame seeds or 1 tsp black sesame powder, plus extra for garnish

10 oz (300 ml) hot water

1 black tea bag or 1 tbsp (5 g) black tea of choice (I recommend Earl Grey or Irish breakfast)

1 oz (30 ml) heavy cream

Honey, to taste

Start your drink prep by crushing your sesame seeds (if using whole ones). You can break them down in a blender, spice grinder, mortar and pestle or just chop them up really finely with a knife—whatever works for you. After they are crushed into a rough, pasty consistency, set your crushed sesame seeds aside for later, or store them in the fridge for 1 to 2 months and use them as needed.

(continued)

Honey, Do You Like Sesame? *(continued)*

Next, heat up the water in your kettle or on the stovetop and then steep the black tea in your mug until it reaches your desired strength, 2 to 3 minutes. While your tea is steeping, you can begin making the honey black sesame cream. In a separate cup, add the heavy cream and honey. Froth or whisk your mixture until it gets thick and pourable, but not so thick that it becomes whipped cream. When using a frother, it usually takes about 2 minutes to get the perfect creamy consistency, and when whisking it can take up to 5 minutes. Then, add your crushed sesame seeds to your honey cream and stir until your mixture has a light gray speckled look.

Finally, add your honey black sesame cream to the top of your tea and garnish it with a few black sesame seeds.

Jasmine Tea Horchatte

1 serving

It's all about balance. The highlight of this tea latte is the traditional Mexican horchata de arroz using jasmine rice (make my Horchata [page 24] with the jasmine rice option for this recipe) and jasmine tea to add a floral pop to its already one-of-a-kind taste. I stumbled upon this fusion of flavors when homemaking horchata for the first time years ago while newly living on my own. I had a sudden craving and happened to have all the ingredients for horchata in the kitchen. The difference was that the only rice I had was jasmine instead of the original long grain. I immediately googled to see if it was "okay" to use. I found an article that said not only was it okay, but it would also add a unique aroma. Since then, I've only used jasmine rice in my horchata and I highly recommend that you try it out, too!

10 oz (300 ml) Horchata (page 24 or store-bought will work)
2 oz (60 ml) hot water
1 jasmine black tea bag or 1 tbsp (5 g) jasmine black tea leaves
Ice
Cinnamon stick, for garnish

Start your drink prep by making your Horchata (see my recipe on page 24 or skip this step if you are using store-bought).

Begin preparing the tea latte by making your black tea shot. Combine the hot water and your black tea in a heat-safe glass and let it steep until it reaches your desired strength. Let the tea shot cool for a few minutes before adding it to the horchata. To a separate glass, add your ice and horchata and top it with your tea shot. To create the layered effect, you can pour your tea shot over the back of a spoon *very* slowly or over an ice cube. Top off your horchata tea latte with a cinnamon stick and enjoy!

The Vegan Thai Iced Tea

1 serving

A delicious vegan alternative to the beloved Thai iced tea, this recipe uses ChaTraMue brand's Thai Tea Original mix, which you can find online or in almost any Asian grocery store for the classic orange Thai tea color. While the recipe that you'll find in most restaurants uses sweetened half and half, this rendition uses a dairy-free alternative in two places: the coconut base at the bottom and coconut cream on top.

10 oz (300 ml) hot water

2 tbsp (10 g) orange Thai tea leaves (I recommend ChaTraMue's Thai Tea Original)

1 oz (30 ml) coconut whipping cream

2 tbsp (30 ml) condensed coconut milk, divided

1 oz (30 ml) coconut milk

Ice

Begin by brewing your Thai tea. I would recommend doing this ahead of time so your tea is chilled by the time you're ready to serve. You can even make a big batch so you can enjoy it all week long! In a heat-safe glass, combine the hot water with the Thai tea leaves and stir to make sure the hot water reaches all of the tea leaves. Let it steep for 2 to 3 minutes and then strain out the tea leaves.

Now, let's make the condensed coconut milk cream. In a cup, combine your coconut whipping cream and 1 tablespoon (15 ml) of condensed coconut milk. You can whisk or froth this until it gets thick and pourable, but not so thick that it becomes scoopable whipped cream. When using a frother, it usually takes about 2 minutes to get the perfect creamy consistency, 3 minutes if you're using an electric beater and 5 minutes if you're whisking by hand.

To your glass, add the remaining 1 tablespoon (15 ml) of condensed coconut milk and the coconut milk and stir until there are no more clumps. Then, add the ice followed by your Thai tea—make sure to leave about 1 inch (2.5 cm) at the top of your glass for the coconut cream. Top off your Thai tea with the condensed coconut milk cream.

The Sunnyside

1 serving

This balance of citrusy, floral and bitter flavors was inspired by the classic gin and tonic, my favorite cocktail of *all* time. The vibrancy of the blood orange juice in contrast to the effervescence of the bubbly tonic will show you the sunny side of life. Tonic can be a bit of an acquired taste so if it's not your thing, use your favorite sparkling water or soda as a substitute. Cheers, my friends!

*2 black tea bags or 2 tbsp (10 g) black tea of choice
(I recommend English breakfast)*

2 oz (60 ml) hot water

2 oz (60 ml) fresh blood orange juice

Ice

6–8 oz (180–240 ml) tonic water

Blood orange slice, for garnish

Begin by brewing your black tea shot. Add your tea bags to the hot water in a heat-safe glass and let the mixture steep for 2 to 3 minutes. Let the tea shot cool for a few minutes so it does not dilute the ice in your drink too much.

Next, add the blood orange juice and tea shot to the bottom of a separate glass, add as much ice as you want, then add tonic water to the top. Last, garnish your tea tonic with a thin slice of blood orange.

Home Café Tip

When garnishing, slide your slice of blood orange along the wall of your glass so you can see all the details of the drink. Against the bubbly sparkling water, the blood orange will almost look like a piece of stained glass.

The Earl of Grapefruit

1 serving

Wanna go on a picnic? I have the perfect drink for you to take. It's light and summery but grounded by the pop of the bergamot in the Earl Grey. I use ruby grapefruits in this recipe to give it that light pink color and sweet bitterness, but feel free to use whatever grapefruit you can find. Wherever you're drinking this spritzer, be sure to "cheers" yourself or "cheers" your friends because you deserve it!

2 Earl Grey tea bags or 2 tbsp (10 g) Earl Grey tea leaves

2 oz (60 ml) hot water

1 tbsp (15 ml) sweetener of choice (I recommend honey or agave)

2 oz (60 ml) freshly squeezed grapefruit juice

Ice

Grapefruit wedge, for garnish

8 oz (240 ml) sparkling water

Begin by brewing the Earl Grey tea shot. Add your tea bags to the hot water in a heat-safe glass and let it steep for 4 to 5 minutes. Then add your sweetener and the grapefruit juice and mix them until they are well combined.

Next, add ice to a separate glass, then slide a thin wedge of grapefruit between the ice and the wall of your glass. Follow that up with some sparkling water, leaving 1 to 2 inches (2.5 to 5 cm) of room at the top. Top off the drink with your tea shot and watch as the clear sparkling water slowly turns to a sparkly amber.

Tea Berry Affogato

1 serving

This just might be the easiest recipe in this chapter—it only has three ingredients, but it tastes like a *dream*. A variation of the classic affogato, this combination pairs a classic milk tea taste with berries, the perfect sweet and tart complement to its decadence. You will *definitely* want a second serving. This treat was inspired by the Tea Berry ice cream at Franklin Fountain in Philadelphia, Pennsylvania. They took it off their menu for several years, but they recently put it back on due to popular demand, so this affogato is an homage to that tried-and-true classic. I hope you enjoy it as much as I do!

3 oz (90 ml) hot water

*2 black tea bags or 2 tbsp (10 g) black tea leaves of choice
(I recommend English breakfast or Earl Grey)*

¼ cup (40 g) frozen mixed berries

2 scoops vanilla ice cream

Begin by brewing your tea. In a heat-safe glass, combine the hot water with your black tea and let it steep until it reaches your desired intensity, 2 to 3 minutes.

Next add the frozen berries to a separate glass. I recommend frozen over fresh berries because when eaten, they have a sorbet-like consistency and add to the frozen aspect of this dessert. To construct your affogato, add your scoops of ice cream on top of the berries and pour the tea into your glass. The frozen berries combined with the ice cream and tea will blend to create a light pink color once it is stirred.

Mango Tango Tea

1 serving

This recipe was born from pure experimentation. When I was younger, juice used to be my beverage of choice—orange, cranberry, guava, mango, passion fruit, you name it—but as I got older, my tastes started to change. Instead of craving the sweet juices from my childhood, my palate started to crave something more complex with a bitter, grounding element and a pop of acid. In this recipe, the black tea is that bitter element and the lime juice is that citrus note. You can enjoy this tea in the comfort of your home and it will immediately transport you to a tropical getaway.

10 oz (300 ml) hot water

*1 black tea bag or 1 tbsp (5 g) black tea leaves of choice
(I recommend Ceylon or Assam)*

1 oz (30 ml) mango juice or nectar

½ oz (15 ml) lime juice

1 tbsp (15 g) sweetener of choice, or to taste (I recommend agave nectar)

Start by brewing your tea. In your mug, combine the hot water and black tea. Let the tea steep until it reaches your desired strength, 2 to 3 minutes. Next, add the mango juice to your tea along with the lime juice and sweetener. This tea is best enjoyed hot but is great iced, too!

Green Tea *Delights*

It is hard to beat a good ol' cup of green tea. Our initial thoughts about tea can sometimes be a little lackluster: tea leaves, hot water, cup. This chapter takes green tea and brings it to new heights, pairing it with delicate sweeteners, fruit juices and frozen delights.

Originating in China and harvested all across Asia (most commonly), the different varieties of green tea are vast and steeped in tradition. Different forms include sencha, Dragonwell, gunpowder, jasmine, genmaicha and Hojicha, among many others. You might be thinking, don't mess with the classics, let tea be tea . . . but this is a great opportunity to switch things up a bit and try different tea combinations, familiar and unexplored. That hot mug of green tea you drink when you're feeling under the weather can also be a green tea snow cone or blended green tea drink. No combination is too crazy. My hope is that the recipes to come will tantalize your taste buds and give you some new ideas for experimenting with green tea.

Before getting into this chapter, the most important tip is to avoid steeping green tea for more than 3 minutes unless advised on the package. Brewing for too long can make the tea bitter and can lead to an unpleasant aftertaste. With all of this in mind, let your green tea speak to you and have fun with it!

My Floral Lady

1 serving

Whenever my family and I would go to dim sum, the first thing that was brought to our table was a piping hot pot of jasmine tea. Most times, the handle would be way too hot, and the tea would be spilling out of the spout onto the white tablecloth. When the tea finally cooled down enough to take a sip, its taste was simple yet so exquisite. This recipe was inspired by those memories and uses jasmine tea as a foundation for the essences of rose and honey.

Honey Rose Syrup

2 oz (60 ml) honey

2 oz (60 ml) water

1 tbsp (4 g) dried rose petals or 1 oz (30 ml) rose water

Tea

10 oz (300 ml) hot water

1 jasmine green tea bag or ½ tsp green tea leaves (I recommend sencha) + ½ tsp dried jasmine flowers

Honey Rose Syrup, to taste

Dried rose petals or jasmine flowers, for garnish (optional)

Begin by making your honey rose syrup. To start, in a small saucepan over medium heat, combine the honey, water and dried rose petals. Stir your mixture until all the honey has dissolved. Then, turn the heat down to low and let your syrup simmer for 5 to 7 minutes, stirring occasionally. This will help your syrup thicken slightly. The longer you leave it to simmer, the thicker it will become. Strain the syrup (if you're using dried rose petals), let it cool and store it in an airtight container in the fridge for up to 2 weeks.

To make your jasmine green tea, combine the hot water with your tea bag or tea leaves. You can do this in a teapot or in your favorite cozy mug. Let the tea steep until it reaches your desired strength. I like to steep my tea for no more than 3 minutes. Finish off your drink by adding as much of the honey rose syrup as you like. Sweetness is subjective, so you get to choose how much or how little you add! Top your tea with some optional rose petals or jasmine flowers and you are ready to take a sip.

The Winter Tropicale

1 serving

There's nothing better than a simple cup of green tea, but if you are looking for a slight variation from the beloved favorite, look no further than The Winter Tropicale. It uses pineapple juice and apricot preserves as a lightly sweet and fruity reprieve from the bite of the green tea. Not only do they add the perfect amount of sweetness, but they are ready-made, so all you need to do is add them in and stir.

1 green tea bag or 1 tbsp (5 g) green tea leaves (I recommend Tencha)
10 oz (300 ml) hot water
1 oz (30 ml) pineapple juice
1 tsp apricot preserves
1 dried pineapple wheel, for garnish

Begin by brewing your green tea. Combine the green tea with your hot water in your mug and let it steep until it reaches your desired strength. I usually like to steep my tea for 2 to 3 minutes or so.

To your green tea, add your pineapple juice and apricot preserves and stir until all the apricot preserves have dissolved. Garnish your tea with a dried pineapple wheel and enjoy!

Home Café Tip

Jams and preserves are a great way to add a sweet, fruity pop to both hot and iced teas. Jams aren't just for toast anymore; there are no limits in your home café!

Strawbasil Float

1 serving

A clean taste with a crisp circumference . . . literally! Get ready to make your own sorbet for this recipe. The good news is that it is *super* easy. I'm not just saying that. The strawberry basil sorbet is a perfectly fragrant complement to the ice-cold green tea. The basil leaves give the sorbet that perfect herby basil flavor, but you can definitely add more if you prefer a more basil-y taste. So, get that blender ready to create this specialty sip!

Strawberry Basil Sorbet

¼ cup (35 g) frozen strawberries

1–2 basil leaves, torn, plus more for garnish

Agave nectar, to taste (optional)

1–2 tbsp (15–30 ml) water, as needed

Float

1 green tea bag or 1 tbsp (5 g) green tea leaves (I recommend Longjing, aka Dragonwell)

8 oz (240 ml) hot water

Ice

1 scoop Strawberry Basil Sorbet

Begin by making the strawberry basil sorbet. To your blender, add the strawberries, basil leaves and agave nectar (if using). Blend it all together until your mixture is completely smooth. The frozen strawberries might be difficult to blend at first, so you may need to add a few tablespoons (15 to 30 ml) of water at a time to help loosen them up. Feel free to scoop and serve the sorbet right away or store it in a freezer-safe container until you're ready to serve. Your homemade sorbet will last for up to 1 month in the freezer.

Continue your drink prep by brewing your green tea. In a heat-safe glass or jar, combine the green tea with hot water and let it steep until it reaches your desired strength. I like to steep mine for 2 to 3 minutes and make a big batch at the beginning of the week, so I can always have iced tea on hand.

Construct the float by adding your ice and green tea to your glass. Top the green tea with a scoop of your homemade strawberry basil sorbet and garnish it with a few basil leaves on top.

Ombré Green Tea Granita

1 serving

I first learned about granitas on the Food Network almost 20 years ago! In an episode of *Everyday Italian*, Giada De Laurentiis made a fruity granita that I just could not take my eyes away from. I can't remember what flavor it was, but it was pink, and it looked so icy and full of flavor. So, when thinking of recipes for this book, one of my immediate thoughts was *"tea granita"*! Here you have it, the gracious green tea pomegranate granita.

*2 green tea bags or 2 tbsp (10 g) green tea leaves
(I recommend gunpowder tea)*

8 oz (240 ml) hot water

1 tsp sweetener of choice (I recommend agave or stevia)

1 oz (30 ml) pomegranate juice

1 tbsp (15 g) pomegranate arils, for garnish

Start by making the green tea granita. First, in a baking pan or metal mixing bowl, combine your green tea with your hot water and let it steep for 10 minutes. This is the exception to the 3 minute steeping limit. Because the green tea will be frozen, it will need a stronger green tea flavor. After steeping, remove your tea bags or leaves and add your sweetener, stirring until it has all dissolved. Let your tea cool for 5 to 10 minutes and then put it into the freezer for 1 hour.

After the hour is up, take your green tea out of the freezer and scrape it with a fork, crushing all the solid, frozen pieces until the mixture becomes snow-like. Your mixture will still be a liquid consistency after the first scrape. Place your soon-to-be granita back into the freezer and continue to scrape every 15 to 20 minutes until all the tea has frozen completely. Be sure to set aside 2 hours or so in total, as you will be scraping your granita over the course of the next hour to get the perfect consistency. You'll know it's ready when it looks like green tea snow! I would suggest enjoying it right when it's ready, but you can keep it in the freezer for up to 5 days, mixing and scraping it once a day or so.

To construct the final product, add the pomegranate juice to the bottom of your glass, then spoon in the green tea granita. The pomegranate will create a red ombré effect from the bottom up as it combines with the green tea crystals. Garnish your granita with some pomegranate arils and enjoy!

Passionate About Green Tea

1 serving

This is the perfect beverage to have in hand while lounging poolside. Passion fruit is the star of the show, delicately blended throughout the tiny ice crystals of the frozen green tea. This recipe is inspired by my go-to order at any boba shop: passion fruit green tea with boba. That familiar taste of the green tea is awakened by the tropical, sweet nectar of passion fruit. It's vibrant, cool and herbaceous. I hope you enjoy this favorite of mine!

Passion Fruit Syrup

2 passion fruits (save 1 slice for garnish)

4 oz (120 ml) water

½ cup (100 g) granulated sugar

Tea

1 green tea bag or 1 tbsp (5 g) green tea leaves (I recommend Longjing, aka Dragonwell)

8 oz (240 ml) hot water

1 cup (225 g) ice

2 tbsp (60 ml) Passion Fruit Syrup (store-bought will work too)

Begin your drink preparation by making your passion fruit syrup. If you are using store-bought, you can skip this step. Start by cutting your passion fruits in half. The slice will reveal a white rind with small black seeds surrounded by a vibrant orange flesh. To release the seeds, take a spoon and scrape out the inside of the passion fruit. Add the seeds to a medium saucepan with the water and sugar. Heat the ingredients over medium heat until all the sugar has dissolved, stirring it often. After all the sugar has dissolved, turn the heat to low and let it simmer for 5 to 7 minutes. The longer you simmer it, the thicker it will be. Take the syrup off the heat and strain out the black seeds (straining is optional, but I prefer to do so). Let your syrup cool and store it in an airtight container in the fridge for up to 1 week.

Begin brewing the green tea. Combine your green tea with the hot water in a heat-safe glass and let it steep until it reaches your desired strength. I like to steep mine for 2 to 3 minutes. Let your tea cool before combining it with the other ingredients. This will ensure that it does not melt the ice too much.

In a blender, combine the ice, passion fruit syrup and green tea. Blend your ingredients together until all the ice chunks have dissolved. Pour the tropical slush into your glass and garnish with a sliver of passion fruit for some added pizzazz.

Herbal *Infusions*

All the recipes in this chapter use herbal, and therefore caffeine-free, teas! If you're worried about getting the jitters or are trying to cut back on caffeine in general, these are a great starting point for crafting your home café. They take tried-and-true classics like mint and chamomile to the newer favorites, like butterfly pea flower tea, on new journeys with sparkling water, milk foams and warm spices.

When I was younger, herbal teas were my parents' go-to to keep me from bouncing off the walls. Along with kid-temperature hot chocolate, my other favorite Starbucks drink was a passion tea lemonade. It was one of the few I was allowed to have since it didn't have caffeine. Since then, herbal teas have held a special place in my heart. They have a delicate first taste, which makes them a great foundation for other flavors or a light accent to bolder aromas.

Just a few quick notes before you fire up the tea kettle—make sure to steep your tea for 4 or even 5 minutes. This is longer than black and green teas and ensures that you are getting the most flavor out of your brew. Next, making big batches of tea is the easiest way to cut down prep time. If you prefer your herbal teas iced, make a big batch at the beginning of the week so you can enjoy it all week long.

The great thing about this chapter is that each of the recipe elements are easy to find and easy to make. I can almost guarantee that you have at least half of the ingredients for each recipe in your kitchen already. Happy brewing!

Corazón del Sol

1 serving

Fresh and fruity! This drink is a take on the *piña jamaica agua fresca*. Jamaica, more commonly known as "hibiscus" in the U.S., can be an acquired taste for some because of its tartness. But the sweetness of the pineapple juice combined with the floral, sour notes of the hibiscus tea and lime juice make for the perfect trio. This drink is colorful, full of flavor and (the best part) super quick and easy to make.

1 hibiscus tea bag or 1 tbsp (4 g) dried hibiscus flowers

2 oz (60 ml) hot water

6 oz (180 ml) pineapple juice

½ oz (15 ml) lime juice

Ice

Lime slice, for garnish

Begin by making your hibiscus tea. In a heat-safe glass, combine your hibiscus tea bag or the dried hibiscus flowers with the hot water. Let it steep for 5 minutes or until it has reached your desired strength. We are going after the deep, vibrant red color of the hibiscus flower. Make sure to let the tea cool before adding it to your drink so it does not melt the ice and thus dilute the drink too much.

Next, add the pineapple juice, lime juice and ice to a separate glass. Then, take the hibiscus tea and carefully pour it over an ice cube or the back of a spoon to create the layered effect. Garnish it with a wheel of lime on top and enjoy!

A Fresh Start

1 serving

With all the freshness of mint and the sweetness of your favorite berries, this herbal iced tea is caffeine-free and adds a little something extra to the usual iced tea experience. For the mixed berry syrup, I prefer to use a frozen mixed berry blend because they keep for longer and can be used for smoothies, sorbets, jams, etc. But you can absolutely use fresh berries if it's what you have or prefer!

Mixed Berry Syrup

*¼ cup (40 g) mixed berries of choice
(fresh or frozen)*

¼ cup (50 g) granulated sugar

2 oz (60 ml) water

½ oz (15 ml) lemon juice

Iced Tea

8 oz (240 ml) hot water

2 sprigs of mint or 1 mint tea bag

Ice

Mixed Berry Syrup, to taste

Sliced mixed berries, for garnish

Mint leaves, for garnish

Start your drink preparation by making the mixed berry syrup. In a medium saucepan, combine the mixed berries, sugar, water and lemon juice. Warm them over medium heat until the sugar dissolves and the berries soften. You'll know the berries are softening when they start to look plumper and can be easily smashed with a spoon or spatula. Once the sugar has dissolved, turn the heat down to low and let it simmer for 5 to 7 minutes. This will help the syrup thicken to the perfect consistency. The longer you let it simmer, the thicker it will be. Next, strain your mixture and store it in the fridge in an airtight container for up to 1 week.

Then, make your mint tea by combining hot water and the mint sprigs or mint tea bag in a separate heat-safe glass. I usually let my tea steep for 3 to 4 minutes. Since this is an iced tea drink, you can make the tea ahead of time so it doesn't melt all of your ice, but that is completely up to you! I usually make a big batch of iced tea at the beginning of the week to have on hand. For assembly, add the ice and mixed berry syrup to your glass, followed by the mint tea. Because the syrup is a thicker consistency than the tea, it should automatically make an ombré effect with a dark purplish color at the bottom and a light green color at the top. Garnish your finished drink with a few sliced berries and mint leaves and enjoy!

Sleepytime Soda

1 serving

Chamomile isn't just for bedtime anymore! This tea sparkler will have you floating on an effervescent, chamomile cloud. The longer I do home café, the more I realize that almost anything can be a syrup. That's what inspired this recipe. The delicately sweet chamomile syrup combined with the lightly tart raspberry sorbet is something to be marveled over. Another great thing about this float is that it is caffeine-free but still has a bright pop of flavor.

Chamomile Tea Syrup

2 oz (60 ml) water

2 chamomile tea bags or 2 tbsp (10 g) dried chamomile leaves

¼ cup (50 g) granulated sugar

Soda

Chamomile Tea Syrup, to taste

Ice

8 oz (240 ml) sparkling water

1 scoop raspberry sorbet

1–2 chamomile flowers, for garnish

Start your drink prep by making the chamomile tea syrup. First, to a small saucepan, add the water and chamomile tea and heat them on medium until the chamomile has steeped for 2 to 3 minutes in the hot water. Once your water turns a light yellow color, remove your tea bag and add the sugar, stirring often. Once all the sugar has dissolved, turn the heat down and let it simmer for 5 to 7 minutes. Once your mixture has thickened, take it off the heat, let it cool completely and store it in an airtight container in the fridge for up to 1 week.

To your glass, add the chamomile syrup, ice and sparkling water and top your drink off with a scoop of raspberry sorbet. Garnish it with a few chamomile flowers and enjoy!

Pretty in Purple

1 serving

The combination of the blue butterfly pea flowers and red rose syrup work together to create this lavender dream! Are you intrigued? Butterfly pea flowers are naturally bright blue flowers native to Thailand that are not only known to offer a bunch of health benefits, but also add a pop of color to anything they're combined with. While the pea flowers don't have a strong taste on their own, they can be combined with flavors (like rose) to instantly transform any soda, latte or cocktail.

Rose Syrup

¼ cup (50 g) granulated sugar

2 oz (60 ml) water

1½ oz (45 ml) rose water or 3 tbsp (12 g) dried rose petals

A few drops of red food coloring or beetroot powder

Tea Latte

2 oz (60 ml) hot water

1 tbsp (5 g) dried butterfly pea flowers

8 oz (240 ml) milk of choice (I recommend oat or almond)

Rose Syrup, to taste

Dried rose petals, for garnish

Start your drink prep by making the rose syrup. In a small saucepan, combine the granulated sugar, water, rose water and red food coloring. Heat it over medium heat until the sugar has dissolved and the mixture starts to slightly thicken. It usually takes 5 to 7 minutes. Let your rose syrup cool to room temperature, strain it (if you used dried rose petals) into an airtight container and store it in the fridge for up to 2 weeks.

Next, heat up your water to make the butterfly pea flower tea shot. To your hot water add the butterfly pea flowers and let them steep for 2 to 4 minutes in a heat-safe glass. Watch your mixture turn from a light blue to a deep blue color . . . it is so mesmerizing! While the tea flowers are steeping, heat up your milk with a steamer, in a small saucepan over the stovetop on medium-high heat until it comes to a light boil or pop it in the microwave for 2 minutes. Then, froth your milk if you're in a foamy mood.

To your mug, add your rose syrup, butterfly pea flower tea and steamed milk. When you pour in your milk, your drink should transform into a dreamy lilac color. Garnish your tea latte with some dried rose petals and sip away!

A Ginger Swig

1 serving

This tea is an instant hug. The coziness of the ginger, cinnamon and cloves paired with the apple juice makes for the most soothing sip. If you take a glance down at the instructions, it might be the *easiest* drink in this whole recipe book—just dump the ingredients in the pot and you're already halfway there. While these flavors scream "holiday," this ginger tea is perfect for any time of year.

8 oz (240 ml) water
2 oz (60 ml) apple juice (I recommend unfiltered)
1 thumb of ginger, sliced
1 cinnamon stick or a dash of ground cinnamon
2–4 whole cloves or 1 dash of ground cloves
Sweetener of choice, to taste (I recommend agave or maple syrup)

In a medium saucepan, combine the water, apple juice, ginger, cinnamon, cloves and sweetener. Bring your tea to a slow boil, turn down the heat and let it simmer for 5 minutes.

Strain the tea into your mug and enjoy it hot!

Home Café *Happy Hour*

This chapter is a fusion of what you already love about coffee and tea with a boozy twist.

One of my favorite parts about experimenting with different cocktails is testing them out (of course), but also knowing that there are no rules. Yes, this is going to be a metaphor for life. Let this chapter challenge you to think outside the box, push the norm, appreciate the old while not being afraid to try the new and most importantly, follow your instincts. Add the extra squeeze of caramel, do the Tajín rim, use as many limes as you want! You do you.

Another fun part about making your own cocktails is that you can enjoy them in the comfort of your own home or show off your bartending skills when you have friends and family over. It can be so fun to try a new recipe with those you love and even create signature cocktails of your very own. I've found that coffee and tea are great additions to cocktails because they are interesting and unexpected and they are easily accessible ingredients. Think about it . . . you probably already have some type of tea or coffee in your house, so why not add it to ingredients from your home bar?

A few things before home café happy hour starts—a couple of the recipes to come require a shaking element. If you don't have a cocktail shaker, you can find them online or at almost any store that sells kitchen supplies. If you have a mason jar or something similar, that will work just fine! Finally, there are recommendations for non-alcoholic alternatives at the end of each recipe if you are not partaking.

As always, enjoy responsibly and . . . Cheers! Salud! Santé! Prost! Kanpai/ 乾杯! Geonbae/건배!

Good Morning, Tommy C.

1 serving

The classic Tom Collins cocktail gets a wake-up call in this recipe with the addition of coffee liqueur, which lends a subtle suggestion of earthiness to this refreshing tipple. Say good morning to your newest brunch cocktail.

Simple Syrup

2 oz (60 ml) water

¼ cup (50 g) granulated sugar

Collins Cocktail

1 oz (30 ml) gin

1 oz (30 ml) coffee liqueur

½ oz (15 ml) Simple Syrup or agave (optional)

½ oz (15 ml) lemon juice

Ice

6 oz (180 ml) sparkling water

Lemon slice, for garnish

Begin by making the simple syrup. In a small saucepan, combine your water and sugar and warm them over medium heat until all the sugar has dissolved, stirring often. Once the sugar has dissolved, take your syrup off the heat and let it cool. You can store it in an airtight container in the fridge for up to 1 week.

To your highball glass, add your gin, coffee liqueur, simple syrup (if using) and lemon juice and stir until the ingredients are well combined. Next, add your ice and top your drink off with the sparkling water. Garnish your Good Morning, Tommy C. with a wheel of lemon by placing it between the ice and the rim of the glass. Give it a quick stir before drinking and cheers, my friends!

Home Café Tip

The coffee liqueur in this recipe provides a base of sweetness to this cocktail, so the addition of simple syrup is optional. If you'd rather skip making your own simple syrup, you can use store bought or swap in agave syrup, stevia syrup, monk fruit syrup, etc.! Find these alternatives in the baking aisle of your grocery store. If you'd rather enjoy a non-alcoholic version, skip the coffee liqueur and gin and use 2 ounces (60 ml) of coffee (espresso, Cold Brew [page 55], etc.) instead.

The Salted Caramel-Tini

1 serving

The OG espresso martini is a worldwide favorite. It energizes you while giving you the buzz of a classic martini. This recipe adds an interactive element to your drink. The caramel candy on top is meant to be pushed in before enjoying to flavor your drink, or to be munched on in between sips. Since this is your home café, you'll be making the caramel candies . . . but not to worry, it is much simpler than you think and only requires one ingredient. Yes, one! Whether you're starting your night or ending your night with one of these, get ready to enjoy this beautifully balanced libation.

Caramel Candy

⅓ cup (65 g) granulated sugar

Caramel-Tini

1 oz (30 ml) chilled espresso

1½ oz (45 ml) vodka or tequila

1 oz (30 ml) coffee liqueur

A squeeze of caramel sauce

A pinch of salt

Ice

Caramel Candy, for garnish

Start by making your caramel candy garnish. Before you begin, prepare where you will be pouring your caramel. I suggest a baking sheet or other heat-resistant flat surface lined with parchment paper. To make your candies, start by pouring your sugar into a small saucepan over medium heat. After a few minutes, your sugar will slowly start to melt. Stir your sugar every so often to prevent it from burning. Sugar clumps will start to develop, but if you stir your mixture periodically, the clumps will dissolve. It will take about 10 minutes for the sugar to melt completely, and your mixture should be a rich caramel color by the time it's ready to be poured.

This next step needs to be done fairly quickly. I like to keep my pot over a low heat to prevent the sugar from hardening and to also prevent it from burning. You can either pour the caramel straight onto the parchment sheet from the pan, or you can take a spoon and make fun designs like sticks, spirals, circles or zigzags. Once poured, let your caramel candies harden—it should take about 10 minutes. These candies keep best in a cool, dry place for up to 1 week.

(continued)

The Salted Caramel-Tini *(continued)*

To begin making your martini, brew your espresso. I like to let mine sit out or put it in the freezer for a few minutes, so it doesn't over-dilute the rest of your drink when you shake it. Then, to your mason jar or cocktail shaker, add the vodka, chilled espresso, coffee liqueur, caramel, salt and ice. Shake your drink until it is well chilled and strain it into your favorite martini glass. Garnish your martini with your caramel candies and you are good to go!

Home Café Tip

Cleaning up caramel aftermath can be a pain. So, before attempting to scrape off the hard pieces of caramel from your saucepan, instead, fill it up with water, keep it on medium heat and stir it often until the hard sugar dissolves (it will take about 5 minutes). Then, you can pour your sugar liquid out without having to scrub all of the hard caramel off.

You can substitute the alcoholic ingredients for their zero-proof alternatives. If that's not your thing, you can still make the caramel candies and enjoy them in a variety of drinks.

The Magic Margarita

1 serving

This Magic Margarita will put a spell on you. It has a classic margarita taste with the slightly floral addition of the butterfly pea flower tea. The most magical part of this cocktail is the color-changing butterfly pea flower tea that starts out as a vibrant blue and transforms into a deep violet color when poured into the tart and citrusy margarita mix. So, choose your flavor of choice for the rim, cut up some limes and you're already halfway to enjoying this delicious drink!

½ oz (15 ml) hot water
1 tsp dried butterfly pea flowers
Salt, sugar or Tajín for the rim
1½ oz (45 ml) tequila
1 oz (30 ml) orange liqueur (I recommend Triple Sec or Cointreau)
¾ oz (25 ml) lime juice
Ice
Lime wedge, for garnish

Start by brewing your butterfly pea flower tea. Combine the hot water with the dried butterfly pea flowers in a separate heat-safe glass and let them steep for 3 to 4 minutes. Take out the flowers and let the tea shot cool slightly.

Next, rim your glass of choice with salt, sugar or Tajín. Everyone has their favorite!

(continued)

The Magic Margarita *(continued)*

To your mason jar or cocktail shaker, add the tequila, orange liqueur, lime juice and ice and shake it until the shaker gets cold on the outside. Then, strain it into a glass with fresh ice. Last, slowly pour your tea shot over the top of your margarita mixture to create that layered effect, and watch closely as the blue of the tea shot gradually transforms into a deep purple color. Garnish it with a wedge of lime and enjoy!

————————————————————————— *Home Café Tip*

If you don't drink, you can replace the tequila and orange liqueur with lemon-lime soda or sparkling water with added sweetener for a quick limeade. There are also some great zero-proof tequila alternatives out there. Some of my favorites are Ritual and Free Spirits.

Café Disco

1 serving

This drink's namesake comes from the "Café Disco" episode of *The Office* where the whole gang dances and drinks espresso. It inspired me to put a caffeinated twist on one of my favorite cocktails, the gin sour, using matcha in place of Angostura bitters, which adds the perfect green hue and a unique bitterness. Just a few things to note before you shake this cocktail up: For the foamy element of this drink, you can use an egg white or chickpea water, also known as aquafaba, for a vegan alternative. You can also use the full amount of matcha specified down below for a darker green color, or cut the amount in half for a lighter color and taste. Whichever option you choose, you will be sipping on a tart, herbaceous, foamy masterpiece.

½–1 tsp matcha powder, plus more for garnish

2 oz (60 ml) gin

1 oz (30 ml) lemon juice

½ oz (15 ml) Simple Syrup (page 148)

½ of 1 egg white or ½ oz (15 ml) aquafaba

Ice

In a mason jar or cocktail shaker, combine the matcha, gin, lemon juice, simple syrup and egg white. Do a "dry shake" to combine all the ingredients of your soon-to-be gin sour. After a few shakes, add ice to your shaker and shake for about 30 seconds . . . shake it like a Polaroid picture!

Strain your drink into a coupe glass. Your cocktail should be a vibrant or light green color (depending on how much matcha powder you used) and have a thin layer of foam on top. Dust your cocktail with some more matcha powder and enjoy!

Home Café Tip

If you want to skip the alcohol for this recipe, you can substitute the gin for water or lemonade for an instant mocktail. There are also some tantalizing non-alcoholic substitutes on the market. My favorite brands for non-alcoholic gin are Monday and Ritual.

The Mythical Mojito

1 serving

This ginger black tea mojito is simply one of my favorite cocktails of all time. It gets its sweetness from my ginger black tea syrup, which adds some depth to the vivacious minty bubbles. This recipe is inspired by a trip to Puerto Rico I took with my best friend where we learned how to make mojitos and mofongo. It transports me back to those memories and I hope you can make some memories drinking this mojito too.

Ginger Black Tea Syrup

2 black tea bags or 2 tbsp (10 g) black tea leaves (I recommend English breakfast)

2 oz (60 ml) water

¼ cup (50 g) granulated sugar

1 thumb of ginger or 2 slices of candied ginger, roughly chopped

Mojito

½ oz (15 ml) Ginger Black Tea Syrup

½ lime, cut into 4 wedgess

2 mint sprigs, divided

2 oz (60 ml) white rum

Ice

Club soda or sparkling water

Start by making your ginger black tea syrup. To a small saucepan over medium heat, add the black tea, water, sugar and ginger and stir it often until the sugar dissolves. Next, turn the heat down to low and let your syrup simmer until it thickens slightly, 5 to 7 minutes. Strain your syrup to catch the black tea and ginger pieces and let it cool completely. You can store your syrup in an airtight container in the fridge for up to 1 week.

In a glass, add your ginger black tea syrup, 4 lime wedges and the leaves from 1 sprig of mint. Muddle these three ingredients, breaking up the lime wedges and bruising the mint to release its essence, and combining them with the sweet syrup. I like to break a sweat when I muddle my mojitos . . . that's how you know it'll be flavorful! To your minty muddled mixture, add the rum and ice and fill your glass to the top with club soda or sparkling water. Garnish your mojito with the leaves of your second mint sprig. *Salud!*

Home Café Tip

Transform this mojito into a mocktail by leaving out the rum, or substituting it with a zero-proof rum alternative.

Acknowledgments

Thank you to my wonderful editor, Franny Donington, who has been the greatest source of knowledge and support each step of the way. She challenged my scientific writing brain to think more creatively, and I could not have asked for a better partnership. Endless thanks goes to Gaby Jeter of Gaby J Photography, the amazingly talented photographer of this book. I mean, just look at these photos! She breathed life into each coffee, tea and cocktail that you've seen. These two ladies made this book . . . A FREAKING BOOK!

A multitude of thanks to Page Street Publishing. The Editorial Team—Lauren Knowles, Marissa Giambelluca and Will Kiester. The Design Team—Meg Baskis and Rosie Stewart. The Marketing Team—Charlotte Lymann and Jamie Wright. The Production Team—Meg Palmer, Hayley Gundlach and Cassandra Jones.

To my friends and family, a support system like no other: Mom, Papa, Takumi, Uncle B, Aunt Sina, Cherae, Nia, Bibo (and many more)! You encouraged me to keep writing and I am here today because of you. Thank you for always believing in me.

To the fellow drink lovers who have supported me via @ac_homecafé, thank you from the bottom of my heart for sending messages of encouragement my way throughout this process and making my account what it is today. I hope you enjoy every single one of these recipes in your home cafés!

About the Author

Asia Lui Chapa is a drink recipe developer and video creator best known for her Instagram account @ac_homecafé. Since creating simple drink videos at the beginning of the pandemic in March 2020, her reach has transformed into recipe developing and collaborating with various beverage brands across the United States, like Guinness, Captain Morgan and Peet's Coffee.

Before pursuing recipe development and video creating, Asia's work included everything from running reception desks, tutoring psychology students, working as a community crisis counselor and getting a master's degree in legal and forensic psychology. While working in the mental health field by day, she taste-tested and prepped for her drink videos by night, slowly developing a passion she didn't realize she had. The rest is history!

When she's not writing or filming drink videos, Asia loves trying new restaurants, watching *The Office* and *Gilmore Girls* over and over and snuggling with her dog, Bibo Ralph Lui Hori Chapa Jeannin (yes, that's his full name).

Index

A

affogato
  Tea Berry Affogato, 118
  Toasted Coconut Affogato, 43
Almond Brûlée Latte, 28
apple juice, in A Ginger Swig, 144
apricot preserves, in The Winter Tropicale, 127

B

bananas, in Brown Sugar Banana Syrup, 35
basil leaves, in Strawberry Basil Sorbet, 128
Be Bold Brew, 81
berries
  Mixed Berry Bubbly Matcha, 92
  Mixed Berry Syrup, 139
  Tea Berry Affogato, 118
black sesame seeds, in Honey, Do You Like Sesame? 107–109
black tea
  Ginger Black Tea Syrup, 160
  Honey, Do You Like Sesame? 107–109
  Jasmine Tea Horchatte, 110
  Mango Tango Tea, 121
  The Sunnyside, 114
  Tea Berry Affogato, 118
blackberries, in Mixed Berry Bubbly Matcha, 92
blood orange juice, in The Sunnyside, 114
Blueberry Lavender Syrup, 104
Blueberry Lavender Tea Latte, 104–106
The Bright Side, 100
Brown Sugar Banana Latte, 35
Brown Sugar Banana Syrup, 35
butterfly pea flowers
  The Magic Margarita, 155–156
  Pretty in Purple, 143

C

Café Disco, 159
Campfire Iced Coffee, 66
Caramel Candy, 151
caramel sauce, The Salted Caramel-Tini, 151–152
Caramel-Tini, 151
Chamomile Tea Syrup, 140
Cheese Foam Iced Coffee, 73
Cherry Pistachio Mocha, 36
Cherry Pistachio Syrup, 36
chocolate sauce
  Be Bold Brew, 81
  Double Chocolate Matcha Float, 91
  Wake Up, Lavender, 44
Cinnamon Choco-Latte Float, 39
The Classic Cold Brew, 55
The Classic Drip Coffee, 52
The Classic Latte, 20
cocktails
  Café Disco, 159
  Good Morning, Tommy C., 148
  The Magic Margarita, 155–156
  The Mythical Mojito, 160
  The Salted Caramel-Tini, 151–152
cocoa powder
  Cherry Pistachio Mocha, 36
  Tiramisù Espresso Con Panna, 32
  Wake Up, Lavender, 44
coconut, in Toasted Coconut Affogato, 43
coconut milk
  Cinnamon Choco-Latte Float, 39
  Tres Leches Iced Latte, 23
  The Vegan Thai Iced Tea, 113
coconut whipping cream, in The Vegan Thai Iced Tea, 113
coffee. See also lattes
  Be Bold Brew, 81
  Campfire Iced Coffee, 66

Cheese Foam Iced Coffee, 73
The Classic Cold Brew, 55
The Classic Drip Coffee, 52
Cookies 'n' Cream Coffee, 74
Foamy Spiced Maple Café, 59
Gingerbread Cold Brew, 77
Honey Lavender Cold Brew, 78
Honeycomb Coffee, 60–62
Salty Maple Cold Brew Granita, 63–65
Shaken White Mocha Iced Coffee, 69
Spiced Honey Coffee, 56
Ube Coffee Float, 70
coffee liqueur
  Good Morning, Tommy C., 148
  The Salted Caramel-Tini, 151–152
coffee tools, 12–13
cold brew coffee. See also iced coffee
  Be Bold Brew, 81
  The Classic Cold Brew, 55
  Gingerbread Cold Brew, 77
  Honey Lavender Cold Brew, 78
  recipe for, 55
  Salty Maple Cold Brew Granita, 63–65
  store-bought, 13
Collins Cocktail, 148
condensed coconut milk
  Tres Leches Iced Latte, 23
  The Vegan Thai Iced Tea, 113
Cookies 'n' Cream Coffee, 74
Corazón del Sol, 136
cream cheese, in Cheese Foam Iced Coffee, 73
crème sandwich cookies (Oreos), in Cookies 'n' Cream Coffee, 74

D

Double Chocolate Matcha
Float, 91
drip coffee, 52
drip coffee makers, 12

E

Earl Grey tea
    Blueberry Lavender Tea
        Latte, 104–106
    The Earl of Grapefruit, 117
    Honey, Do You Like
        Sesame? 107–109
    Tea Berry Affogato, 118
The Earl of Grapefruit, 117
espresso
    Almond Brûlée Latte, 28
    Brown Sugar Banana
        Latte, 35
    Cherry Pistachio Mocha,
        36
    Cinnamon Choco-Latte
        Float, 39
    The Classic Latte, 20
    Espresso Tónica, 47
    Frozen Horchata Latte,
        24–27
    The Salted Caramel-Tini,
        151–152
    Shaken Maple Espresso,
        40
    Sparkling Espresso
        Lemonade, 48
    Tiramisù Espresso Con
        Panna, 32
    Toasted Coconut Affogato,
        43
    Tres Leches Iced Latte, 23
    Wake Up, Lavender, 44
    Warm & Toasty White
        Mocha, 31
espresso machines, 10
Espresso Tónica, 47
espresso tools, 10–11

F

Foamy Spiced Maple Café, 59
French press, 13
A Fresh Start, 139
frozen drinks
    Cinnamon Choco-Latte
        Float, 39
    Double Chocolate Matcha
        Float, 91

Frozen Horchata Latte,
    24–27
Ombré Green Tea Granita,
    131
Salty Maple Cold Brew
    Granita, 63–65
Sleepytime Soda, 140
Strawbasil Float, 128
Tea Berry Affogato, 118
Toasted Coconut Affogato,
    43
Ube Coffee Float, 70
Frozen Horchata Latte, 24–27

G

gin
    Café Disco, 159
    Good Morning, Tommy
        C., 148
ginger
    Ginger Black Tea Syrup,
        160
    A Ginger Swig, 144
Ginger Black Tea Syrup, 160
A Ginger Swig, 144
Gingerbread Cold Brew, 77
Gingerbread Syrup, 77
glassware, 17
Good Morning, Tommy C., 148
grapefruit juice, in The Earl of
    Grapefruit, 117
green tea
    My Floral Lady, 124
    Ombré Green Tea Granita,
        131
    Passionate About Green
        Tea, 132
    Strawbasil Float, 128
    The Winter Tropicale, 127
green tea granita, 131
guava nectar, in Icy Guava
    Matcha, 96

H

heavy cream
    Cheese Foam Iced Coffee,
        73
    Cookies 'n' Cream Coffee,
        74
    Frozen Horchata Latte,
        24–27
    Honey, Do You Like
        Sesame? 107–109
    Matcha-Misù Tea Latte, 84

Salty Maple Cold Brew
    Granita, 63–65
Tiramisù Espresso Con
    Panna, 32
Tres Leches Iced Latte, 23
herbal infusions
    Corazón del Sol, 136
    A Fresh Start, 139
    A Ginger Swig, 144
    Pretty in Purple, 143
    Sleepytime Soda, 140
hibiscus tea, in Corazón del
    Sol, 136
honey
    The Bright Side, 100
    Honey Rose Syrup, 124
    Lavender Honey Syrup, 78
    Spiced Honey Coffee, 56
Honey, Do You Like Sesame?
    107–109
Honey Lavender Cold Brew, 78
Honey Rose Syrup, 124
Honeycomb Coffee, 60–62
Horchata
    Frozen Horchata Latte,
        24–27
    Jasmine Tea Horchatte,
        110
    recipe for, 24

I

ice cream and sorbet
    Cinnamon Choco-Latte
        Float, 39
    Double Chocolate Matcha
        Float, 91
    Sleepytime Soda, 140
    Strawbasil Float, 128
    Tea Berry Affogato, 118
    Toasted Coconut Affogato,
        43
    Ube Coffee Float, 70
ice molds, 17
iced coffee. See also cold
    brew coffee
    Brown Sugar Banana
        Latte, 35
    Campfire Iced Coffee, 66
    Cheese Foam Iced Coffee,
        73
    Cherry Pistachio Mocha,
        36
    The Classic Cold Brew, 55
    Cookies 'n' Cream Coffee,
        74

Espresso Tónica, 47
Shaken Maple Espresso, 40
Shaken White Mocha Iced Coffee, 69
Sparkling Espresso Lemonade, 48
store-bought, 13
Tres Leches Iced Latte, 23
Ube Coffee Float, 70
Wake Up, Lavender, 44
iced matcha
    The Bright Side, 100
    Double Chocolate Matcha Float, 91
    Icy Guava Matcha, 96
    The Lemongrass Lady, 95
    Mixed Berry Bubbly Matcha, 92
    Sparkling Matcha Lemonade, 99
iced tea
    Corazón del Sol, 136
    The Earl of Grapefruit, 117
    A Fresh Start, 139
    Jasmine Tea Horchatte, 110
    The Sunnyside, 114
    The Vegan Thai Iced Tea, 113
Icy Guava Matcha, 96

J
jasmine green tea, in My Floral Lady, 124
Jasmine Tea Horchatte, 110

L
La Vie En Rose Latte, 88
lattes
    Almond Brûlée Latte, 28
    Brown Sugar Banana Latte, 35
    Cherry Pistachio Mocha, 36
    Cinnamon Choco-Latte Float, 39
    The Classic Latte, 20
    Espresso Tónica, 47
    Frozen Horchata Latte, 24–27
    Shaken Maple Espresso, 40

Sparkling Espresso Lemonade, 48
Tiramisù Espresso Con Panna, 32
Toasted Coconut Affogato, 43
Tres Leches Iced Latte, 23
Wake Up, Lavender, 44
Warm & Toasty White Mocha, 31
Lavender Honey Syrup, 78
lavender petals
    Blueberry Lavender Syrup, 104
    Lavender Honey Syrup, 78
    Lavender Syrup, 44
Lavender Syrup, 44
lemon juice
    Café Disco, 159
    Good Morning, Tommy C., 148
    Lemon Syrup, 48
    Mixed Berry Syrup, 139
    Sparkling Matcha Lemonade, 99
Lemon Syrup, 48
The Lemongrass Lady, 95
Lemongrass Tea, 95
lime juice
    Corazón del Sol, 136
    Icy Guava Matcha, 96
    The Magic Margarita, 155–156
    Mango Tango Tea, 121

M
The Magic Margarita, 155–156
mango juice, in Mango Tango Tea, 121
Mango Tango Tea, 121
maple syrup
    Foamy Spiced Maple Café, 59
    Salty Maple Cold Brew Granita, 63–65
    Shaken Maple Espresso, 40
    Spiced Maple Matcha, 87
marshmallows, in Toasted Marshmallow Syrup, 66
mascarpone cheese
    Matcha-Misù Tea Latte, 84
    Tiramisù Espresso Con Panna, 32

matcha
    about, 83
    The Bright Side, 100
    Double Chocolate Matcha Float, 91
    Icy Guava Matcha, 96
    La Vie En Rose Latte, 88
    The Lemongrass Lady, 95
    Matcha-Misù Tea Latte, 84
    Mixed Berry Bubbly Matcha, 92
    Sparkling Matcha Lemonade, 99
    Spiced Maple Matcha, 87
matcha powder
    The Bright Side, 100
    Café Disco, 159
    Icy Guava Matcha, 96
    La Vie En Rose Latte, 88
    The Lemongrass Lady, 95
    Matcha Syrup, 99
    Matcha-Misù Tea Latte, 84
    Mixed Berry Bubbly Matcha, 92
    Spiced Maple Matcha, 87
Matcha Syrup, 99
matcha whisk, 14
Matcha-Misù Tea Latte, 84
milk frothers, 10–11
mint
    A Fresh Start, 139
    The Mythical Mojito, 160
Mixed Berry Bubbly Matcha, 92
Mixed Berry Syrup, 139
mocha, 44
    Cherry Pistachio Mocha, 36
    mocha, 44
    Shaken White Mocha Iced Coffee, 69
    Warm & Toasty Mocha, 31
Mojito, 160
moka pots, 10
My Floral Lady, 124
The Mythical Mojito, 160

O
Ombré Green Tea Granita, 131
orange liqueur, in The Magic Margarita, 155–156
orange Thai tea leaves, in The Vegan Thai Iced Tea, 113

P

Passion Fruit Syrup, 132
Passionate About Green Tea, 132
pineapple juice
    Corazón del Sol, 136
    The Winter Tropicale, 127
pistachios, in Cherry Pistachio Syrup, 36
pomegranate juice, in Ombré Green Tea Granita, 131
pour-over coffee sets, 13
Pretty in Purple, 143

R

rice, in Horchata, 24
rose petals
    Honey Rose Syrup, 124
    Rose Syrup, 143
Rose Syrup, 143
rose water
    Rose Syrup, 143
    Vanilla Rose Syrup, 88
rum, in The Mythical Mojito, 160

S

The Salted Caramel-Tini, 151–152
Salty Maple Cold Brew Granita, 63–65
Shaken Maple Espresso, 40
Shaken White Mocha Iced Coffee, 69
Simple Syrup, 148
Sleepytime Soda, 140
Sparkling Espresso Lemonade, 48
Sparkling Matcha Lemonade, 99
sparkling water
    The Earl of Grapefruit, 117
    Good Morning, Tommy C., 148
    Mixed Berry Bubbly Matcha, 92
    The Mythical Mojito, 160
    Sleepytime Soda, 140
    Sparkling Espresso Lemonade, 48
    Sparkling Matcha Lemonade, 99
    The Sunnyside, 114

Spiced Honey Coffee, 56
Spiced Maple Matcha, 87
Strawbasil Float, 128
strawberries
    Mixed Berry Bubbly Matcha, 92
    Strawberry Basil Sorbet, 128
Strawberry Basil Sorbet, 128
The Sunnyside, 114
sweetened condensed milk, in Tres Leches Iced Latte, 23
syrups
    Blueberry Lavender Syrup, 104
    Brown Sugar Banana Syrup, 35
    Chamomile Tea Syrup, 140
    Cherry Pistachio Syrup, 36
    Ginger Black Tea Syrup, 160
    Gingerbread Syrup, 77
    Honey Rose Syrup, 124
    Lavender Honey Syrup, 78
    Lavender Syrup, 44
    Lemon Syrup, 48
    Matcha Syrup, 99
    Mixed Berry Syrup, 139
    Passion Fruit Syrup, 132
    Rose Syrup, 143
    Simple Syrup, 148
    Toasted Marshmallow Syrup, 66
    Vanilla Rose Syrup, 88

T

tangerine juice, in The Bright Side, 100
Tea Berry Affogato, 118
tea infusers, 14
tea kettles, 14
tea lattes
    Blueberry Lavender Tea Latte, 104–106
    Honey, Do You Like Sesame? 107–109
    Jasmine Tea Horchatte, 110
    La Vie En Rose Latte, 88
    Matcha-Misù Tea Latte, 84
    Pretty in Purple, 143
    Spiced Maple Matcha, 87
tea tools, 14

tequila
    The Magic Margarita, 155–156
    The Salted Caramel-Tini, 151–152
Tiramisù Espresso Con Panna, 32
Toasted Coconut Affogato, 43
Toasted Marshmallow Syrup, 66
tonic water
    Espresso Tónica, 47
    The Sunnyside, 114
Tres Leches Iced Latte, 23

U

Ube Coffee Float, 70

V

Vanilla Rose Syrup, 88
The Vegan Thai Iced Tea, 113
vodka, in The Salted Caramel-Tini, 151–152

W

Wake Up, Lavender, 44
Warm & Toasty White Mocha, 31
white chocolate sauce, in Double Chocolate Matcha Float, 91
white mocha sauce
    Shaken White Mocha Iced Coffee, 69
    Warm & Toasty White Mocha, 31
The Winter Tropicale, 127